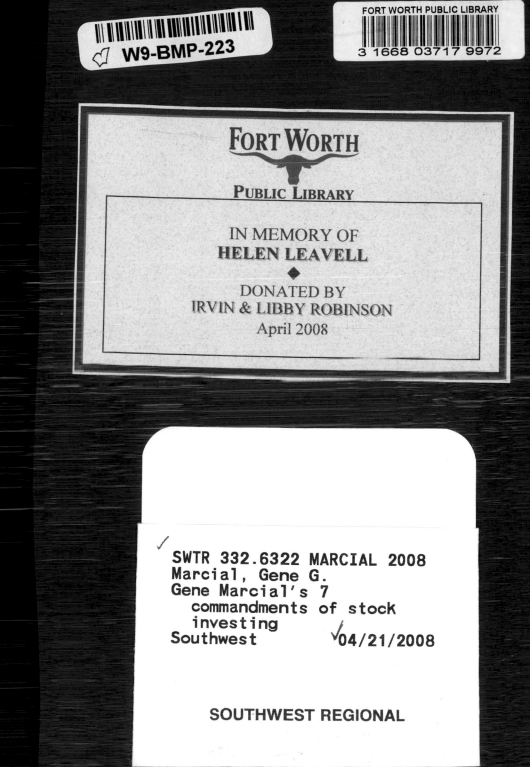

Gene Marcial's

7

COMMANDMENTS
OF
STOCK
INVESTING

Vice President, Publisher: Tim Moore
Associate Publisher and Director of Marketing: Amy Neidlinger
Executive Editor: Jim Boyd
Editorial Assistant: Pamela Boland
Development Editor: Russ Hall
Digital Marketing Manager: Julie Phifer
Marketing Coordinator: Megan Colvin
Cover Designer: Ingredient
Managing Editor: Gina Kanouse
Copy Editor: Karen A. Gill
Proofreader: Erika Millen
Indexer: Lisa Stumpf
Senior Compositor: Gloria Schurick
Manufacturing Buyer: Dan Uhrig

© 2008 by Pearson Education, Inc.
Publishing as FT Press
Upper Saddle River, New Jersey 07458

This book is sold with the understanding that neither the author nor the publisher is engaged in rendering legal, accounting, or other professional services or advice by publishing this book. Each individual situation is unique. Thus, if legal or financial advice or other expert assistance is required in a specific situation, the services of a competent professional should be sought to ensure that the situation has been evaluated carefully and appropriately. The author and the publisher disclaim any liability, loss, or risk resulting, directly or indirectly, from the use or application of any of the contents of this book.

FT Press offers excellent discounts on this book when ordered in quantity for bulk purchases or special sales. For more information, please contact U.S. Corporate and Government Sales, 1-800-382-3419, corpsales@pearsontechgroup.com. For sales outside the U.S., please contact International Sales at international@pearsoned.com.

Company and product names mentioned herein are the trademarks or registered trademarks of their respective owners.

Printed in the United States of America

First Printing March 2008

ISBN-10: 0-13-235461-6
ISBN-13: 978-0-13-235461-5

Pearson Education LTD.
Pearson Education Australia PTY, Limited.
Pearson Education Singapore, Pte. Ltd.
Pearson Education North Asia, Ltd.
Pearson Education Canada, Ltd.
Pearson Educatión de Mexico, S.A. de C.V.
Pearson Education—Japan
Pearson Education Malaysia, Pte. Ltd.

Library of Congress Cataloging-in-Publication Data

Marcial, Gene G.
   Gene Marcial's seven commandments of stock investing / Gene G. Marcial.
      p. cm.
   ISBN 0-13-235461-6 (hbk. : alk. paper) 1. Stocks. 2. Speculation. 3. Investments. I. Title.

HG6041.M353 2008
332.63'22—dc22

2007044777

To Kristi,
for her love, support, and
encouragement.

Contents

Foreword

Gene Marcial and I have something in common: We wake up every morning and go to sleep each night thinking about stocks. When you are as focused and obsessed as we are, you develop certain tenets about investing.

Obviously there are a lot of ideas about how to make money in the stock market, some more serious than others. I always got a kick out of reading various theories that have popped up—especially some of the wackiest that assume you can predict the overall market direction. One of my favorites, which is probably thirty years old, is the hemline indicator, also known as the "bull markets and bare knees theory." Supposedly when hemlines go up, so do stocks. When they go down, so do stocks.

I'm a big football fan, so the old Super Bowl indicator is another gem. It says when a team from the American Football League (AFL, which is now AFC) wins the championship, it's going to be a down year. If a National Football League (NFL, which is now NFC) team wins, the market will be up, up, up.

Popular theories can also apply to individual stocks. During the madness of 1929 and its aftermath, investors "watched the tape" religiously. Common wisdom was that if a stock declined it should be sold, quickly. If it went up, it should be bought. In 1934 a book called *Security Analysis* by Graham and Dodd offered an escape from the crowd sentiment. Instead of viewing stocks as pieces of paper, Ben Graham and David Dodd saw them as shares of a business whose value, over time, would correspond to the value of the enterprise. They urged investors not to pay attention to the tape—but to focus on the businesses beneath the stock certificates. Ben Graham laid out a methodological basis for picking stocks. He looked for businesses with a margin of safety—he said an investor should insist on a big gap between what he was willing to pay and his estimate of what a stock was worth. These two pioneers invented the profession of security analysis, in which I was trained. Studying under these "hot shots" in 1950 was the seminal event for another investor, Warren Buffett, who reaped great benefits from adhering to their principles.

What Gene Marcial has done in this book is to capture his own experiences from listening and writing about stocks for 30 plus years. This period has seen bad markets, good markets, and volatile markets. Graham and Dodd personified the capricious movements as "Mr. Market," who shows up every day to buy or sell. "Mr. Market" is a strange fellow, subject to all sorts of unpredictable mood swings that affect the price at which he is willing to do business. Gene shares with us his seven commandments that are a practitioner's handbook, honed by his wealth of experience, and that will help navigate around "Mr. Market."

These are solid, well-developed commandments that have reaped substantial benefits to those who have adhered to them. By doing the research, removing the emotion from your investment decisions, focusing on your best ideas, being a long-term investor, not timing the market, and buying businesses at a discount to their intrinsic value, you will improve your chances of financial success. We call this intrinsic value the Private Market Value, and we focus on a catalyst, or event that will help surface the value in the company.

There are many catalysts, but a telling one, which Gene mentions in this book, is the repurchase of shares. When management is buying back stock, the analyst questions what the rationale is. Is the repurchase to offset dilution from stock options? To share with shareholders some form of compensation? Or are they buying below their estimate of intrinsic or what we at Gabelli call Private Market Value? So tracking a company or an individual's purchase of shares, particularly when done without the threat of greenmail or the threat of a takeover, can prove to be a very practical approach to begin the process of looking at an idea.

Gene is also a student of market history. Momentum investors have at times made tons of money, but at other times have been flattened in some classic bubbles. I never understood the rush to invest in index funds. Supposed "investors" would continue to buy regardless of the price—and without even knowing the names of the companies they are investing in! From my experience, long-term, fundamental stock selection is the key to creating wealth or preserving it.

Gene has a great nose for stocks. We had been long-term holders of Aztar for our clients. We owned enough to require it to get registered with the Nevada Gaming authorities. The company operated the Tropicana Casino and Hotel in Vegas and Atlantic City. Our focus was its crown jewel, the 34 underutilized acres on the strip in Las Vegas that we thought would be attractive to other gaming operators. Gene was right there in June of 2005 and included Aztar in his column. Noticing the takeover activity in gaming stocks, he picked up on Aztar's takeover potential and recommended it at $31.50 per share. On March 13, 2006, the following year, Pinnacle Entertainment offered $38 cash per share and a bidding war ensued. Three other bidders kept topping each bid over the next two months, and Columbia Entertainment ultimately bought the company for $54.00 in cash per share.

Gene's goal is to change individual stock investors' mind-sets to help them to take advantage of opportunities. Armed with his seven commandments, an investor can go confidently and intelligently into the market. Let his wisdom of over three decades help you become a successful investor.

—*Mario Gabelli*
    Chief Investment Officer of Gabelli and Co.
    Chairman and CEO of Gamco Investors Inc.
    Member of the *Barron's* Roundtable

Acknowledgments

My thanks to my many trusted reliable news sources on Wall Street who helped make this book a sharp advocate of intelligent, realistic, and gutsy market maxims for the individual investor.

I am very grateful for the support of my close friend and mentor, Seymour Zucker, a former senior editor at *BusinessWeek* magazine, who encouraged this endeavor from the start. He was kind enough to read the first draft of this book. He was my supervising editor at *BusinessWeek*, prior to his retirement in 2005, who steered the "Inside Wall Street" column to where it is today. I credit him for inculcating more energy and judicious perspective into the column. He has done the same for this book.

Special thanks to John A. Byrne, executive editor of *BusinessWeek*, for his early support. I could not have proceeded with confidence with this book without his kind encouragement.

I also want to acknowledge the support of Jim Boyd, executive editor of Pearson Education, Financial Times Press, and Wharton School Publishing, whose advice and assistance very much contributed to the completion of the book. He encouraged me several years ago to embark on this project, and I am grateful for it. I also want to express my appreciation for the kind and expert assistance of some of the other editors at Pearson, FT Press, and Wharton School Publishing, among them Amy Neidlinger, Russ Hall, Julie Phifer, Gina Kanouse, and Betsy Harris.

A special thanks to Patricia O'Connell, who was among the first who helped spark the idea for this book. I am also indebted to John Cady, Susan Zegel, and Yvette Hernandez for their invaluable assistance in helping me in my information and data research.

—Gene G. Marcial, November 2007

About the Author

Gene G. Marcial is a senior writer and columnist at *Business-Week* where he writes the market-moving column "Inside Wall Street." Prior to that he wrote the Heard on the Street column for the Wall Street Journal. He is also the author of the book *Secrets of the Street: the Dark Side of Making Money* (McGraw-Hill, 1995), a candid exposé of the machinations of Wall Street insiders. Marcial works and lives in New York City.

To the Reader

I have been avidly analyzing the stock market for more than 30 years, first as a market columnist for *The Wall Street Journal* for seven years, followed by 26 years at *BusinessWeek* magazine, where I continue to write the "Inside Wall Street" column. Fortified with all that experience and seasoning, I felt I had to write this book for investors who have been bewildered and frustrated by Wall Street.

I joined *BusinessWeek* on August 3, 1981, purposely to write the "Inside Wall Street" column after its previous writer resigned to join a Wall Street firm. I would not have left *The Wall Street Journal*, where I was a happy camper, had I not been offered the opportunity to write *BusinessWeek*'s premier market column. In *The Journal*, I was one of three who wrote the columns "Heard on the Street" and "Abreast of the Market." Previous to writing for *The Wall Street Journal*, I was a copy editor at the Associated Press-Dow Jones Economic Report for three years.

This book is a summation of what I have observed about the stock market in all those years—interfacing with hundreds of analysts, investment managers, financial consultants, brokers, and professional investors. I have compressed my experience and observations into seven maxims that I believe sum up what investors should understand—and should do—about the market and picking stocks.

I am sharing with you the novel ways I use in my column to beat the market. I write about 150 to 170 stocks every year. Not all of them come out winners, of course. But, on average, they have outperformed the pros hands down. In the past ten years, since 1997 when *BusinessWeek* started tracking the performance of the weekly "Inside Wall Street" column, my picks bested the S&P 500, Dow Jones Industrial Average, and Russell 2000.

The idea of writing this book had been kicking around in my head for several years, following the publication of my first book, *Secrets of the Street: The Dark Side of Making Money*, in 1995. The market continued to move so fast, however, that it was quite fanciful to think I could come up with another timely and relevant book amid the sharp changes happening in the marketplace and on Wall Street, which had inspired a flood of books about the market.

Nonetheless, watching the market gyrate through all kinds of hoops and hoopla that drove investors into great panic—as if the world were coming to an end—finally convinced me to get on with this book. It is no secret that fear and greed rule the market. When fear mounts, most people panic, and they go into an uncontrolled selling mode. And when good news pervades, the greed factor takes over, and people chase after stocks for fear of being left behind. I have witnessed this fear-and-greed syndrome time and time again.

Knowing how to use the fear-and-greed factor is the first step to making money on Wall Street. But it is only the first step. A careful reading of this book provides the investor with the know-how to beat the market.

—*Gene G. Marcial*
New York City
January 14, 2008

Introduction

There are plenty of ways to make money in the stock market, but clinging to mainstream thinking or so-called conventional wisdom is not one of them. This book's seven commandments are definitely out-of-the-mainstream thinking, aimed at conditioning your mind to always look at the stock market as a market of opportunity. These seven commandments should clear your mind of old market clichés and encourage you to jump on hidden opportunities to make money.

Panic is the enemy of the investor. The stock market offers great chances to make money when the big institutional investors are running for the exits and driving stock prices down. Ditto, when the institutions are driving up stock prices as they go on a buying rampage. That, in essence, is what the first commandment of this book is all about.

The second commandment addresses most investors' favorite strategy: diversification. It has universal investor appeal. Most folks feel safer when their portfolios sport a diversified, "low-beta" look, consisting of stocks of every stripe. My advice: Don't. Do not diversify. Instead, concentrate the bulk of your stock market capital in a few stocks to reap robust profits. Diversification might make you feel safe. After all, that is what the many market mavens have been drilling in your head all these years. But what diversification guarantees are mediocre returns. The banks are a safe place to store money. The stock market is not. To reap rich rewards from the stock market, you must bear some risks.

My third commandment goes against the widely accepted norm of going with the winners. My view: Let the winners gallop into the sunset without you. Instead, go after some of the prominent stocks that have stumbled or fallen. When a company's stock has crashed, the market almost invariably has discounted all of the bad news. And that's just the time when you can pick up real bargains from the casualty list.

The fourth commandment rejects the popular notion that "timing is everything." That might be valid in other aspects of life, but it's not in the stock market. Timing the market can screw up your portfolio. I debunk the concept that investors should time their entry or withdrawal from the market based on the economic cycle or seasonal or historical events. Timing is part of the "herd mentality" syndrome, which, more often than not, leaves an investor in negative territory.

The fifth commandment: Nobody wins like an insider does. By thinking and adopting the ways of an insider, an outsider can also win big. This book provides a formula for trading on the inside and unravels the mystique surrounding insiders. My first book, *Secrets of the Street: The Dark Side of Making Money*, revealed the clever ways insiders use to make millions. They were mostly of the illegal kind. But there are ways to get valuable information like an insider without getting enmeshed in illegal trading. Adopt the insider's ways— and win.

The sixth commandment tackles the unknown—the investors' fear of what they aren't familiar with. Little-known companies, like the biotechs, as well as the shares of foreign companies, offer great opportunities. This sixth maxim familiarizes you with the world of hidden stocks, where many still-undiscovered opportunities have not been brought to light. The pros who focus on this universe of practically invisible stocks make their pile when they attract liquidity or buyers to them. Don't fear the unknown. Know and understand it as a real opportunity.

The final chapter's seventh commandment advocates long-term investing. It is, after all, the best investment strategy. This chapter looks at how the pros profit from their long-term investing, and it recommends seven "sweet stocks" for the next seven years.

One principle that underlies the entire book's seven commandments is the widely known but seldom followed adage, "Buy low, sell high." Even hard-nosed investment pros dismiss that advice because they consider it too simple. The truth is, that strategy is difficult to put into effect. It is more complex when you attempt to execute and translate it into reality. It requires all the guts and courage to practice it—to know just when a stock is actually selling at a low price—and to have the discipline and conviction to buy it.

This book is not about predicting the direction of the market or forecasting the next meltdown or "melt-up." It exposes the basic misconceptions that have victimized investors all these years. Despite the flood of books published every year and the stream of countless newspaper and magazine articles and market newsletters, unrealistic concepts still saddle multitudes of investors with losses. This book can help you avoid being victimized and make you a winner in the market.

January 14, 2008

COMMANDMENT 1

Buy Panic

"Buy only what is being thrown away."

—John Templeton, legendary investor and founder of the Templeton Funds

Welcome to the world of panic, the big generator of market meltdowns. It is tsunami-like: When panic grips the stock market, waves of selling overtake practically every stock. There is panic on the upside as well, which drives up stocks in a frenzy. This chapter gives you an idea of how to react to such meltdowns. It explains how investors should confront panic in the marketplace. The thesis: Panic can be your ally.

When investors jump on the bandwagon of fear in times of panic, don't be a follower. Investors should not join the running of the panicky bears or bulls. Panic begets loss of logic. And when logic goes, investors become vulnerable to jittery mob mentality. That is a sure pathway to pain.

On February 27, 2007, when the Chinese stock market crashed almost without warning, U.S. investors went into a panic, causing the Dow Jones industrial average to plunge 416.02 points, or some 3.3 percent, to 12,216.24. Many of the investors I called the next day for a reaction had one common answer: "We sold." Panic was in the air.

In less than a month, however, the market regained much of what it had lost. The Dow had trekked back up to 12,481.01 on March 23, 2007. The market gained more energy and continued to climb, hitting an all-time high of 14,000.41 on July 19, 2007. The bulls ruled again. However, as the sub-prime mortgage problem appeared to worsen, fresh fears mounted over concern that the sub-prime meltdown appeared to have infected credit markets around the world. Again, panic gripped the market on August 9, 2007, driving down the Dow Industrials 387 points, or 2.8 percent, to 13,270.65. The bears took control—but not for long. On September 18, the Dow posted its biggest one-day percentage gain since 2003, soaring 335.97 points, or 2.51 percent, to 13,739.39.

The Federal Reserve Board was behind the big bounce: It cut the federal-funds rate by half a percentage point to 4.75 percent, which exceeded most economists' prediction of a quarter-point cut.

The two market crashes during February and August of 2007 were followed by robust rallies, which were tremendous opportunities to make money. Another opportunity to bargain-hunt came up on November 12, 2007, when the Dow slipped below 13,000, to 12,987.55, as investor confidence was rattled by the continued fallout from the credit-market crisis sparked by the mortgage maelstrom. It was the first time the Dow had closed below 13,000 since August 16, 2007. By November 16, 2007, the Dow had rebounded to 13,178. For sure, it is likely to bounce around some more but I would be very surprised if it doesn't jump back to an upward trend.

These crashes paled in comparison to how scared investors were during the horrible 9/11 terrorist attacks in 2001. Justifiably, panic gripped the nation. The New York Stock Exchange shut down operations to prevent panic trading from overwhelming the market. When the Big Board reopened a week later, droves of investors rushed to sell.

Uncontrolled Fear

Indeed, the 9/11 attacks were one of the darkest moments in U.S. history. The market world looked like it was headed for total chaos. The entire nation, along with the rest of the world, convulsed and panicked. And, not surprisingly, many of the institutional investors rushed to protect their investments and issued sell orders—indiscriminately, in most cases.

Such dire situations almost always provide opportunity for steeled and pragmatic investors to make handsome profits. Investors with the wherewithal to snap up stocks when nobody wants them wind up counting rich rewards. Investors had ample opportunities to pick up real bargains. Let me recount how the market crashed in the aftermath of 9/11 and then picked up to climb to record highs three years later.

The market was already teetering before that tragic September 11, 2001. The Dow stood at 9,162.23, down from 11,337 on May 21, 2001 in the aftermath of the bursting of the tech bubble and an economic slowdown. On September 11, the stock market operations became disrupted by the terrorist attacks, and the markets shut down for a week. Pandemonium reigned when the market reopened, and by September 21, the Dow had tumbled by about a thousand points, to 8,235. Practically all stocks were for sale and, despite the bargains to be had, few people had the spirit to go bargain hunting. The market remained a barren source of good news, with small rallies failing to find legs to stand on. The rest of 2001 was a lost cause as the market continued to inch lower, but again that period represented a "Buy Panic" opportunity to some steel-hearted investors. Indeed, by early 2002, the market was showing some signs of life, and on March 19, 2002, the Dow had cranked up to 10,635.25. That period from mid-September of 2001 to March opened a window of opportunity for those who had hunted for bargains.

By March 11, 2003, equities again tumbled in a big way: The Dow plunged to 7,524.06. Was it another buying opportunity for the panic buyers? Indeed, it was, for right after the market's dive in March, the Dow started to race up again, hitting 10,453.92 on December 13, 2003. By that time, the air seemed to have lifted, with the market once again feeling unbounded.

After climbing from late December of 2003 through March of 2005, the Dow didn't do much the rest of the year. 2006 was a turning point for the market. It was the year when the Dow started to hit new record highs. On December 27, 2006, the blue-chip barometer jumped to 12,510.57, marking the beginning of a robust rally, despite the more than 400-point decline in February 2007. It started packing higher, striking new record highs almost every week. On July 19, 2007, the Dow soared to a heady, all-time record high of 14,000.41.

Two kinds of panic spook investors. One is panic that affects the entire market, created by national or global events. Inflation, recession, massive earnings declines, or national calamities are forces that produce total market chaos. The second type is panic associated with specific events that impact a particular stock or group of stocks or industries. In such cases, the crash is stock specific or industry specific.

I discuss examples of these kinds of breakdowns, such as the ones instigated by government probes into the use of accounting fraud in some of the major corporations, resulting in the ouster of top executives. In the process, the shares of those companies were severely beaten down.

To take advantage of the awesome declines, investors must plot a clear strategy to seize opportunities during a market panic, which usually comes out of the blue.

Expect the Unexpected

The first principle that investors have to adhere to is quite simple: Be prepared. Investors must be psychologically prepared for any surprise the market can deliver. Part of preparedness is assuming the market can tumble sharply at any time. Corollary to that: Always assume the market can mount a sudden big rally.

After you drill that into your head, that these surprises can besiege the market without warning, you are ready to take on panic.

First of all, assuming that you are already invested in the stock market and you want to take advantage of the bursts of market activity, you need to have a cash reserve. Cash reserves should be from 10 to 20 percent of your portfolio.

That brings us to the next step: Prepare two lists of stocks. The first list to keep handy is of stocks you want to own for the long haul. If you already have them in your portfolio, mark them as the stocks you should buy more of. These are the stocks that, when they tumble in price, you would want to snap up to add to your holdings. The second list should consist of stocks you own but that have already produced handsome gains, and that you would be willing to sell when the market goes on a buying rampage. The reason to sell them is so you can augment your cash fund.

Armed with these two lists of stocks, an investor will have a clear mind as to what to do when a panic situation hits the market. He or she will be free of fear about any trouble in the marketplace. The Buy Panic commandment will, in truth, free you of the jitters that normally afflict investors in times of market volatility.

This is not to suggest that you will engage in short-term trading. On the contrary, this maxim encourages building a long-term portfolio and, with an ample cash reserve, fortifying it whenever panic times hit the equity market. It suggests for you to build a stronger long-term portfolio, by increasing the number of the good stuff you have in your portfolio when opportunities come knocking.

There are a couple of ways of taking advantage of the market's dysfunction in times of panic. When the market starts selling off, watch which of your favorites are getting a whacking. Because you have owned these stocks for a while, you have an idea whether they are being unjustifiably pounded, based on their fundamentals. Any drop of 5 to 10 percent or more should be enough to inspire you to buy more shares. If the stocks drop to anywhere near their 52-week lows, that should also alert you to buy. Also, consider your cost at the time you first bought them. If their prices are lower than your original buying prices—or even if they're just about even—consider them a bargain.

Let us look at the flip side. When the market is rapidly pumping up, as it was on September 18, 2007 when Federal Reserve Board Chairman Ben Bernanke cut the federal-funds rate by a half a percentage point, you should sell the stocks you listed as disposables or potential profit sources. Remember: You have to sell stocks that have given you sufficient profits so you can build up your cash reserves with which to buy more of your favored stocks.

When you embrace the Buy Panic commandment, you will— strange as this might sound—look forward to the market's periodic bouts of panic. You will finally see the stock market as nothing more than a bastion of opportunities.

Now, how do you know that you are holding stocks that are solid enough to keep and buy more of? One important basic requirement is homework/research. A big part of homework is reading up on the market and stocks. Be an earnest reader of anything that has to do with investing and the markets. Newspapers and magazines are a good start. After you develop the habit of reading the business and investment sections of periodicals, you will become more informed about stocks, their prices and trading patterns, their high and low points, and price-earnings ratios. Make it a habit to read books on equity investing and the markets. You will be familiarizing yourself with a big part of the stock market. These books are not trivial; they are essential information about a part of the business world where you can make money.

The Internet is a big arsenal of information about companies, their backgrounds, and every aspect of their businesses. Yahoo.com, Google.com, and AOL.com quickly come to mind, in addition to Web sites of newspapers like *The New York Times, The Financial Times, The Wall Street Journal,* and *Investors Business Daily. BusinessWeek Magazine* provides more than 350,000 companies worldwide in its Company Insight Center, as a free resource on the Web, at http://investing.businessweek.com/research/company/overview/overview.asp.

Of course, there is always the direct approach. Most corporations are willing to send out information directly to future and present investors. The majority have Investor Relations Offices that handle these matters of interest for investors. Contact the companies directly by phone, letter, or through their Web sites.

Searching for information might already be part of your routine if you are invested in the market. If you aren't yet comfortable or experienced enough to know what to buy or sell to practice the Buy Panic rule, there is one simple and easy way to do it. You will rarely fail if you start concentrating on the major big cap stocks. These are the **blue chips**. Start with the 30 components of the Dow Jones Industrial Average, or the most widely held stocks, including General Electric Co., Boeing Co., AT&T Inc., Citigroup Inc., Coca-Cola Co., and ExxonMobil Corp., to name just a few.

The main reason I suggest them is because it is easier for investors to understand these companies because most of them have widely known brands or franchises.

During market meltdowns, these companies get hit as much as the small-cap stocks, and sometimes even harder. Although they have vast resources and are triple-rated companies by the credit rating agencies, they are as vulnerable to the panicky swings of the market as the small fries are. The large-cap and widely followed stocks are definitely the logical candidates to start with in practicing the Buy Panic commandment.

For investors who work for or are associated with publicly traded companies, the most convenient way to start applying the Buy Panic maxim is to buy employer stock. With your knowledge of the company, you likely feel comfortable and confident about buying your company's shares—assuming that it is a relatively well-managed company. Closely follow the stock through the company Web site or internal sources of information. After you get a handle on its stock, watch how it trades. When one of those market crashes takes place, make sure you are on the ready to grab any opportunity and buy more should the stock drop sharply.

Playing the market with your employer's stock is a practical way of testing your patience and nerves in practicing the Buy Panic commandment. Ownership of stock in your company familiarizes you with the challenges that confront investors day to day. You will find yourself keeping tabs of the company's growth, outlook, and quarterly earnings guidance. Investors in effect are students of companies, and exam time is when the market starts jerking around to test nerves— and decision-making prowess.

A good example of a stock that challenged investors is Goldman Sachs, the premier U.S. investment bank. Even the Wall Street giant took a beating when the credit squeeze troubles grabbed the headlines. If you played the panic game with its stock, you easily could have piled up significant profits. Let's see how that worked.

Shares of Goldman Sachs, one of the most profitable and rapidly growing Wall Street houses, traded as high as $233 a share in June

2007. Its stock was knocked when the subprime mortgage troubles erupted. The height of panic selling caused by the credit problems started on August 13, 2007, and Goldman's stock tumbled to $177.50 a share that very day. In just a couple of days, the stock got pounded even harder, pulling the stock down to $164. For the Buy Panic investor, that would have been a perfect buying point. Knowing Goldman Sachs background and resources, would you have thought that the company was in danger of getting into serious trouble because of the subprime mortgage mess? The stock behaved like it was in serious trouble, and many investors, including some of the institutional investors, did sell the stock in their usual panicky way.

At $164 a share, the Goldman Sachs stock was a pure bargain, selling at just 6.8 times projected 2008 earnings of $23.90 a share, compared with a price-earnings ratio of 10 in June. A month later, on September 18, the market mounted an unexpected giant rally, driven by the Fed's federal-funds rate cut. Goldman Sachs stock was among the market's giant winners. The stock closed that day at $205.50. Just about a week later, the stock continued to fly, to $210—and rising. That was a 46-point jump in just over a month, had you practiced panic buying. On October 31, 2007, Goldman Sachs' stock hit a 52-week high of $250.70.

Now that you are fully prepared for panic, the complex stock market becomes a bit simpler. In sum, opportunities abound if you are alert enough during times of panic. True, you can lose money under certain and unusual circumstances. But by obeying the Buy Panic commandment, your chances of winning are almost clear and nearly predictable. And when you become proficient at it, panic won't even enter your mind. You will be sufficiently mentally prepared, so sudden market jerking won't confound you anymore. In fact, you will welcome panic on Wall Street because you now know how to profit from it.

Buying Stocks in Trouble

Now let us look at some professional investors who are believers and practitioners of the Buy Panic maxim when it affects specific stocks or industries.

One of these investors is value investor John E. Maloney, who is chairman and chief executive officer of M&R Capital Management, Inc. Like a classic "panic player," Maloney looks for companies in trouble and whose stocks have tumbled to their lows. He jumps at opportunities to buy shares of such companies—after analyzing their balance sheets, operating margins, and cash flow, to make sure they have good chances of surviving or recovering from whatever ails them at the moment.

Maloney likes to recall what John Templeton said when he addressed a group of investment managers several years ago: "I love it when great companies get into trouble." Thus did Templeton indicate that, indeed, he was a panic buyer.

The October 1987 crash affected the entire market. Maloney hurriedly bought shares of his favorite blue-chip stocks that got swept down by the panic-sellers: Pepsi-Cola (PEP) and Dart & Kraft (DKR), which was later acquired. Those stocks rewarded him well when he sold four years later at about triple the price he had bought them.

Maloney, who cofounded M&R Capital in 1993 after more than 30 years on Wall Street as an analyst and investment banker, spends a lot of time going over about 40 stocks a week to scout for attractive stocks that panicky investors dumped. Among those he came across in 2006 were two high-profile large-cap companies that became overnight villains on Wall Street: American International Group (AIG) and Tyco International (TYC).

AIG, one of the world's giant insurance organizations, isn't a company you would expect to be a candidate for panic buyers. Its reputation worldwide as a leader in the insurance industry has made it a glamour stock for some time. Its 2006 revenues totaled $113.2 billion, with its life and general insurance business accounting for 85 percent.

Maloney bought shares of AIG on March 23, 2005, at $56.32 a share—weeks after New York State Attorney General Eliot Spitzer (now New York's Governor) and the Securities and Exchange Commission started investigations into the use of its nontraditional insurance products and certain assumed reinsurance transactions. AIG admitted to committing several accounting mistakes. Most of the problems at AIG stemmed from weak internal controls in accounting for derivatives and related assets.

"I bought shares of AIG when everybody else was panicking—the extensive probe that was being conducted didn't bother me much," says Maloney. He sensed that AIG'S earnings power was "massive" and that the problems being investigated were "manageable." Maloney figured that, in the end, the whole problem ultimately would cost AIG only $1 per share in earnings.

Trading as high as $77 in 2004, the stock fell to $49.90 at the height of the 2005 inquiry. Maloney's purchase of AIG shares at $56 a share was timely—not too far off the stock's 2005 bottom. Aware of AIG's vast assets, strong revenue growth, and solid earnings, Maloney felt confident about the company's future. By December 18, 2006, the stock had jumped to $72.81. Although Maloney had chalked up a sizable profit again, he continued to hold the stock. On December 14, 2007, at the height of the subprime debacle, the stock got caught in a web, and had plunged to $55. However, Maloney remains steadfast in his belief that AIG will climb to even greater heights—to probably around $90 a share in a year or so. Analysts figure AIG will earn $6.50 a share in 2008. On that basis, Maloney forecasts that by 2012, AIG could earn $10 to $11 a share. That will bring the stock to cloud nine, in the 90-100 zone, says Maloney.

The probe into AIG's operations culminated in a major management shakeup that resulted in the resignation of AIG's long-time CEO Maurice "Hank" Greenberg, a write-down of earnings from 2000 to 2004 totaling almost $4 billion, and a write-down of shareholders' equity of $2.26 billion. AIG also incurred after-tax charges totaling $1.15 billion to settle its numerous regulatory problems, and $1.19 billion to increase loss reserves. After all the adjustments, 2006 earnings totaled $14.1 billion, or $5.88 a share, up from $10.5 billion, or $3.77 a share, versus 2004's earnings of $9.8 billion or $3.75 a share. AIG was able to recoup much of its competitive edge even after a bumpy environment. To alleviate shareholder concerns as a result of the probe, AIG announced the repurchase of $5 billion worth of its shares in 2007 as part of a board-approved $8 billion share buyback program. It also increased dividends at a 20 percent annual rate for the foreseeable future. On October 3, 2007, AIG's stock closed at $68 a share. AIG'S former CEO Hank Greenberg is considering launching a proxy fight to regain his post, according to rumors in the industry. On November 9, 2007, *Forbes* magazine said, if successful, Greenberg would oust the board that had forced him to resign. Stay tuned on this one.

Tyco International was another stock that panicky investors dumped when everything seemed to have gone wrong in 2002 for the big conglomerate. Tyco's operations include fire-protection systems, flow control equipment, underwater communications and power cables, disposable medical supplies, and printed circuit boards. Investors bailed out because of a financial scandal surrounding its former Chairman and CEO Dennis Kozlowski.

Maloney bought shares on June 6, 2002, at $14 a share, when the company became one of the most mistrusted and spurned on Wall Street. The stock traded as high as $63 a share in 2001, but by the following year, the stock plummeted to just $10.10 a share. The investigation into the company's financial mess during Kozlowski's reign started on September 13, 2002, when the SEC filed civil fraud charges against Kozlowski, Tyco chief financial officer Mark Swartz, and chief legal officer Mark E. Belnick. The SEC accused them of failing to disclose multimillion dollar, low-interest loans they took from the company. In some instances, loans were never repaid. The men were also accused of selling Tyco shares valued at millions of dollars while their self-dealing maneuvers remained undisclosed. On June 17, 2005, Kozlowski was convicted of looting more than $600 million from Tyco, spent on lavish parties, fancy and expensive art, and an opulent $30 million Manhattan apartment that featured a $6,000 shower curtain and a $500 umbrella stand. Tyco's former chief financial officer Swartz was convicted for the same crime. Both were sentenced to 25 years in prison.

It was obvious that Kozlowski and his cohorts had committed fraud and looted the company, but Maloney figured that the company's assets, including some pieces of property appraised separately, had a total value far larger than the stock's price then. He estimated that on a sum-of-the-parts valuation, the stock was worth $40 a share. By March 5, 2007, Tyco traded at $30 a share.

It was at about that time in early March that I wrote a story in my "Inside Wall Street" column in *BusinessWeek*, suggesting that Tyco was a timely and cheap buy before the company's "three-way spin-offs." Owning 100 percent of the three companies was a big bonus for Tyco shareholders, my column said.

The new management team—led by Chairman and CEO Edward Breen—that replaced Kozlowski's gang apparently also figured the same valuation. In January 2006, the directors approved a plan to split the conglomerate into three separate publicly traded companies. Tyco split into three in June 2007.

Tyco shareholders received 100 percent of its two units: the healthcare and electronics divisions. Their allocated shares depended on how many Tyco shares they owned. The original company, Tyco International, would retain its fire and security unit, plus the engineering products and services division. By October 3, 2007, Tyco International traded at $44. Tyco Electronics, with the symbol TEL, traded at $35 that date. The healthcare unit, which renamed itself Covidien Limited (COV), traded at $41. Covidien makes plastic products for surgical use. In sum, shareholders of Tyco before the split ended up in a win-win situation: Their original Tyco had jumped from $30 to $44, and in effect their Tyco Electronics and Covidien shares were pure bonus.

Maloney figured that each of the three Tyco companies would strive to expand its respective horizons to enhance shareholder value. With the so-called "conglomerate discount" taken off their backs, each company was no longer burdened by the image of a stodgy company, and each became more flexible and ambitious to achieve its respective goals.

Maloney's buy-on-panic strategy has worked well for his company. Since 1998, Maloney's M&R Capital outperformed the S&P 500 index, except for 2006 when his gross returns of 13 percent were outscored by the S&P 500-stock index's 15.8 percent gain. Mahoney's largest gain was in 1999; his portfolio garnered a heady gain of 32.6 percent, versus the S&P 500-stock index's 21 percent gain.

Distress Investing

Distress investing is another side of panic buying. Some people say that distress investing is similar to the strategy of vulture investors. The approach is the same and the results similarly gratifying. Investors take advantage of a precipitous drop in a stock's price, or a sizable decline in the business and growth of a company.

In other words, the distress-investing player scouts for companies whose businesses have practically collapsed, driving their stocks way down. Usually the companies that distress investors look for are in greater trouble than those that panic investors, like Maloney, invest in.

It is worth repeating here that individual investors aren't expected to do what institutional investors do because they don't have the resources that the professional investors have to pursue strategies like distress investing. But individual investors do have recourse to cutting into these kinds of deals by paying attention to what the distress investors do and go after. Usually, you can find out what these distress players are up to from their filings with the SEC, which categorically state their intentions. For instance, if you know that a person like Martin D. Sass focuses on distress investing, you could simply screen filings by M. D. Sass to determine what kinds of stocks he has been buying. Investor service companies in Washington, D.C. specialize in finding out what these investors have filed. Invariably, newspapers and magazines get hold of them, too, and publish the information. *Barron's*, Bloomberg News, and Reuters usually report these types of stock holdings. Newspapers like the *Wall Street Journal* and *The New York Times* also publish such filings when they involve well-known investors, such as Carl Icahn, Nelson Peltz, George Soros, or Martin D. Sass.

It is a good idea for individual investors to track what these distress investors are buying, but you have to be nimble and quick because distress investors are like race-car drivers: They move fast and act decisively almost at whim. Because their deals end up publicized in the media, it is easy to keep track of them. But again, you have to do some research into what these investors are buying to make sure you are in step with their thinking.

Sass in particular has become an expert at investing in distressed companies. In 1972, he founded MD Sass, a multipronged investment outfit that manages several hedge funds and various investment portfolios. The company's hedge funds invest mainly in financial equities, real estate securities, and risk arbitrage deals. With assets under management of $10 billion, Sass is able to invest where most investors fear to tread. He finds value in companies that others have given up for dead or are on the brink of financial collapse.

One of Sass's prized deals involved Leaseway Transportation Corp., which provides trucking and related services in the U.S. and Canada. Sass invested a total of $20.8 million, on which he made a handsome 60 percent profit in two years. A colorful cast of characters became involved in trying to take control of Leaseway. Among the participants: activist/corporate raider Carl Icahn, Michael Milken's now-defunct but once influential Wall Street bank Drexel Burnham Lambert, Citigroup, and transportation mogul Roger Penske. The genesis of this deal got some publicity, so it is an example of how individual investors could have gone along for the ride, which turned out to be a profitable one.

The story began in June 1987 when buyout firm Citicorp Venture Capital launched a leveraged buyout (LBO) bid for Leaseway for $650 million. Leaseway's two primary businesses were auto hauling—mainly for General Motors, Chrysler, and Toyota—and logistics services, which managed third-party transportation systems. The leveraged buyout deal, LBO, funded by Drexel and Bankers Trust Company, involved $380 million of bank debt, $192.5 million of 13 percent senior subordinated debentures, and $5 million of equity from Citicorp (which is now Citigroup) and Drexel. Drexel Burnham was then flying high from the mighty clout and influence of financier Michael Milken, who was known as the "junk-bond king" in the 1970s. He was indicted on 98 counts of racketeering and securities fraud in 1989. Pleading guilty to six securities law violations, he was sentenced to ten years in prison, but was released after less than two years.

Things turned sour in 1988, a year after the LBO. Leaseway's sales for its auto-related business started to skid because of a severe economic slowdown. Fierce competition from other haulers helped push Leaseway into a financial squeeze. The huge debt that the company incurred because of the 1987 LBO exacerbated its financial woes. The result: Leaseway failed to make interest payments on its 13 senior subordinate debentures.

That failure drove Leaseway into bankruptcy. When it filed for Chapter 11 protection in December 1992, it had 12-month revenues of $753 million and earnings before interest taxes, depreciation, and amortization (EBITDA) of $130 million. Enter the company's creditors—Credit Agricole, the biggest holder of the debentures, and corporate raider Carl Icahn. Before long, the two started battling for more secure positions. But for more than three years, they could not agree on a reorganization plan or an out-of-court settlement to divide the spoils.

That was when the wrangling caught the eye of Marty Sass, having followed the series of unsuccessful negotiations between the banks and bondholders. Sass started accumulating a substantial stake in Leaseway's bonds. At about that time, in late 1992, an exasperated Icahn was trying to get out of the situation and looking for someone to unload his entire bond stake for about $60 million. By then Sass had become the second largest bond holder. By the fall of 1992, Credit Agricole and Icahn were still at loggerheads—and remained at a standstill.

Sass became actively involved. He raised his stake to assume control. Then he made sure that, as the second largest bondholder, his own trusted lieutenant, James B. Rubin, a senior managing director at MD Sass Investor Services, was appointed chairman of the Official Creditors Committee. In that position, Rubin had the responsibility of coordinating efforts in devising a prepackaged Chapter 11 Plan of Reorganization. The next thing Rubin did was negotiate and get on behalf of bondholders substantially all of the company's common stock in return for the bonds.

When Leaseway emerged from bankruptcy in late 1993, it listed its stock on the NASDAQ. That is when the individual investor could have cut into the deal and purchased shares of the reorganized Leaseway. Sass filed papers with the SEC reporting his purchase of shares of Leaseway. The stock traded then at $8. For the panic or distressed players, buying Leaseway after the bankruptcy would have been the ideal buying point because normally investors don't want to touch a company that just came out of bankruptcy. That puts a lid on the price of the stock, so invariably, the shares of once-bankrupt companies remain undervalued. Despite the unpleasant taint associated with bankruptcy, companies that emerge from it are free of old troubles and are more lean and efficient. That is what reorganization does. The debts are paid off and new management steps in.

Rubin joined Leaseway's new board on January 1995. "We wanted to make sure that we acted as a catalyst to maximize the value of Leaseway's common shares," says Sass, in explaining Rubin's getting a board seat. Sass started accumulating shares of Leaseway when it got on NASDAQ, raising his stake to 24 percent. And, as in the case of other companies that had come out of a Chapter 11 reorganization, Leaseway emerged from bankruptcy as an underpriced stock.

Leaseway's intrinsic private-market value was more than the price of the stock. With Leaseway out of the woods, Sass sought to maximize the value of the company by selling it. Leaseway entered into talks with Roger Penske, chairman of Penske Truck Leasing Co. After tedious negotiations, Leaseway's board of directors, on March 15, 1995, approved the sale to Penske Truck Leasing at $20 a share—a 52 percent premium over the previous day's closing stock price. Marty Sass's hard work paid off handsomely.

Here's the lesson that Marty Sass learned from this deal: You can be a latecomer at a party and still leave with the grand prize. Sass realized that patience and determination paid off, but planning and strategy helped seal the deal.

Investors who are able to discipline themselves into buying shares when the market is in a panic, learn to understand value—from tracking how the market prices fluctuate under varying circumstances. Buying a stock when fear is prompting others to sell and selling when greed energizes them to buy is a great learning experience in valuing stocks.

Buying stocks when everybody else is in a panic leads to another principle: concentrated investing. The pros that use the panic-buying strategy have to concentrate their capital in just a few stocks. Diversifying is out of the question.

The book's next commandment, "Concentrate. Diversify Not," explains the merit of concentration versus diversification. Portfolio diversification is a universally popular strategy whose appeal is misguided. The next chapter explains why.

COMMANDMENT 2

CONCENTRATE. DIVERSIFY NOT

"Our policy is to concentrate holdings. We try to avoid buy-ing a little of this or that when we are only lukewarm about the business or its price. When we are convinced as to attrac-tiveness, we believe in buying worthwhile amounts."

—Warren Buffett, in a letter to Berkshire Hathaway
   Shareholders (1978)

Diversification is a lazy man's game. If you are a passive investor and care little for powerful results, diversification is your can of alphabet soup. This chapter advocates portfolio concentration versus diversification.

The widely popular strategy of diversifying a portfolio has ardent followers. and to some investors, particularly the large institutional investment managers, diversification is a handy way of deploying their assets. But for the individual investor, I argue that portfolio con-centration rather than diversification is the better way to bring home solid profits from the stock market. Like Warren Buffett, I oppose the idea of "buying a little of this or that." I advocate buying plenty of shares of relatively few companies to gain maximum returns.

Cruise-Control Strategy

Diversifying one's portfolio is an honored rule in stock investing, a strategy with strong universal appeal. Let me explain first why diversification is such a widely followed strategy. One reason: It is a simple way of getting fully invested with minimum effort. How much brain power do you need to pick, say, 100 stocks from the various sectors of the economy? Usually a diversified portfolio consists of stocks representing almost all industries, such as aerospace, airlines, banking, energy, retailing, technology, pharmaceuticals—you name it. You end up with a laundry list of stocks of every stripe. Diversification is a cruise-control kind of strategy, with a portfolio on limited speed.

Diversification's many advocates say it is a safe type of investing that protects a portfolio from crashing. The theory goes that if one industry is declining, it will be offset by another industry that is on the incline. But this not true. In any powerful market crash, all groups go down. Some stocks might not go down as much as others, but they do decline. Witness what happened when the market crashed on August 9, 2007, when the Dow dropped 387.18 points, or 2.83 percent, to 13,270.68. Almost all stocks were hit.

On the upside, diversification at best produces average results. You will do as well as the overall market—no better, no worse. If a portfolio's components can't go up together, the returns can only be average. In other words, the very principle of stocks balancing each other can only deliver unspectacular results.

This is the reason why actively managed portfolios often outperform the diversified. Institutional money managers can afford to go with diversified portfolios because it's a convenient way for them to deploy their clients' hundreds of millions or billions of dollars in all sectors of the economy—and hope for the best. Remember: The basic goal of the institutional investors is to safeguard their clients' money—to preserve their capital. Diversification, they believe, achieves that goal. But they should know that the rewards will be underwhelming.

Individual investors can do better by scuttling diversification. What am I suggesting? I argue that, for individual investors, a far superior strategy is to pack your portfolio with well-picked stocks. A few potential home-runners are all you need to best the market and stack up handsome returns. It isn't true that nondiversified portfolios are in danger of delivering poor returns in times of market crises, because there is no substitute for strong stocks to make your portfolio fly. When you find a stock you think will be a big winner based on its fundamentals or other factors, invest more of your stock market capital in it. Don't do the Noah's ark type of investing, where all animals are brought in no matter how fast or slow they move. Individual investors should not settle for mediocrity. Buffett, at one of Berkshire Hathaway's annual meetings, described diversification as a "protection against ignorance. It makes very little sense for those who know what they're doing."

The big question, of course, is what stocks to pack into your portfolio. How can you be sure the stocks you choose will outscore the market? Later in this chapter, we examine how the practitioners of this strategy excelled with their concentrated portfolios. In the meantime, let us look at how best to concentrate your portfolio.

Basic Research Is Vital

Let's say that you already have a stock portfolio. Choose the standouts among the stocks you own, like those that buck the trend in down markets. If you have stocks in the portfolio that continue to be losers, drop them. For those who are invested, say, in mutual funds or index funds and want to seek greener pastures by investing in individual stocks, the same rules I enumerate on how to find the right stocks also apply.

The newcomers to investing in individual stocks need to do basic research, first of all, about the market and stocks. One way is to consult a stockbroker who would be able to supply some research material on stocks. You don't have to buy whatever the broker or his research analysts are pitching. But you should seek their help in acquainting you with the market and some stocks. You could start with just a stock or two. After you have done that, then the advice we provide people who already own stock portfolios will apply. But it is important for the novice to read up on individual stocks and the market and do research and learn basic fundamentals of the marketplace before plunging into equity investing.

One important way to judge a stock is price performance over at least a five-year period. If the stock is young and has been around for just a few years, its quarterly performance would be enough to gauge relative performance. By looking at a stock in this context, you will get an idea of whether it has the stamina for the long drive or will become tired over some distance. Stocks bounce around, but when you study their behavioral pattern and their correlation with the market, you will see some connection or disconnection. Typically, the market's behavior influences stocks. When stocks are beaten down by the regular run of bad news, such as the market tumbling because of, say, a spike in consumer prices or a jump in the number of jobless people, you should put them in your "watch list" for further observation. If these stocks consistently react badly to bad news, consign them to the "waiting to be sold" list. You don't need weaklings in your portfolio.

On the other hand, a stock that stands up to bad news and rises on its own steam needs to be nurtured and kept. Buy more shares—a lot more—of such stocks. Investors should pay attention to the stocks that show consistent strength. An important element to evaluating stocks is consistency. If a stock doesn't react positively to good market news, ditch it. However, if the stock also ignores bad news—news it should be susceptible to in a bad way—give the stock another chance.

It is a good "defensive" sign if a stock is able to absorb negative events. No stock is perfect, but a stock can possess both qualities—rising on good news and standing still or, even better, rising on bad news. Rare is a stock that performs that way consistently. So if a stock demonstrates that kind of uncommon quality, grab more shares.

Another reason why a stock would be a candidate for concentration is if it beats analysts' earnings and sales forecasts on a regular basis. It isn't an easy task for a company to beat forecasts year after year. But some of them do. If a company sustains that kind of strength, it's a must-buy. If a stock fails to respond positively to an upbeat flow of earnings or sales surprises, there must be a reason. Check how consistently that has happened. It's worrisome if a stock makes a habit of reacting in that manner. If it does that only occasionally, there must a reason behind it. One could be leaks ahead of the earnings announcement, which presumably boosted the stock a few days earlier, or even a day ahead of the press release on the results. Close monitoring of such stocks is necessary to determine whether the stock belongs in your portfolio.

Analysts look for a lot more reasons to recommend stocks, including dividend payouts, steady and strong cash flow, appeal and popularity of products or services, leadership in its markets, management integrity, and the rate of sales and earnings growth. You can also look for such factors, but you would need to do a lot more research, which might require the help of financial advisers or brokers who cater to individual investors, such as Charles Schwab and T. D. Ameritrade. But the big investment houses catering mostly to institutions also have working units that serve the individual investors, including Fidelity, T. Rowe Price, Merrill Lynch, Bear Stearns, Wachovia Capital, Piper Jaffray, A.G. Edwards, Oppenheimer, Raymond James, Edward Jones, and many others. It is helpful to individual investors if they can get reports of analysts on particular stocks. These reports aren't infallible, but they do aid in guiding investors about companies or stocks they know little about. Brokerage houses make such reports available to their clients. Your friendly broker might be able to help in this regard.

When Should You Sell?

One question that always comes up is when investors should sell. A lot of books and articles have been written on this subject, because selling is as important as buying. When to sell is a tough question for many reasons. But it is less of an issue if you are a long-term investor, which I would advise everybody to be. Given a longer time horizon of, say, five to ten years or even longer, the issue of when to sell becomes less of a problem. Long-term investors put a long-term target on their holdings, so the up and down wiggling of the market is less of a concern. If the stocks of the long-termers depreciate in value during times of volatility, the investors have more time and patience to wait it out.

However, the time to sell, even for the long-term investor, is when the stock has met its price target. But even then, investors can continue holding the stock if everything is going well with the company. The investor can pare his holdings and wait to repurchase when opportunity knocks—when the stock's price tumbles. Certain problems might arise while you are holding the stock, which can require a decision as to whether to sell. The only reason to bail out is if the basic fundamentals of a company have changed, or if your personal interest in the stock, for whatever reason, has diminished.

What if the stocks you chose to concentrate on turn out to be losers? True, you could make a mistake, but the risk of that happening is not as high as you think. Presumably, you have studied these stocks and have learned how they have performed over time. In other words, these stocks have a track record on which you based your judgment in buying the stock. That, plus presumably other favorable factors you considered, is important. But at times things change. Assess the magnitude of the change or changes. Then decide. Each case is different, of course, and requires varying answers.

The strategy is to focus investing on stocks that have fallen but that had been winners in the past. But if the stock continues to fall, you should re-examine the facts about the company. There have been many cases when such things did occur, but ultimately the stocks rebounded in large measure because what hit them was a nonfundamental issue from which the company was able to recover.

A case in point involved Greg MacArthur, president of investment outfit Viewpoint 2000 and a dyed-in-the-wool long-term investor, who put a buy recommendation on Polycom (PLCM) when it was languishing at $16 a share in July 2005. A few days later, however, Polycom, a major maker of high-quality videoconferencing systems, dropped a couple of points after a large Wall Street investment house put a sell recommendation on the stock. At the same time, Polycom was being targeted by the short sellers. They were betting that the company would go bust. MacArthur bought shares and paid $15 a share, convinced that Polycom was on the right track in a growth industry.

Polycom is a worldwide leader as well as a "pure play" in the growing videoconferencing business. The rising cost and time-consuming inconvenience of travel have made videoconferencing an attractive alternative for many cost-conscious businesses. MacArthur figured that by integrating the broadest array of high-definition video, wired and wireless voice, and content in its videoconferencing system, Polycom was positioned for growth.

The stock didn't go anywhere for months after MacArthur concentrated his capital in the stock. Soon, many other institutional investors turned negative because of the persistent short-selling in the stock. But MacArthur patiently stayed with the stock, pegging a

12-month price target of $22. His optimism paid off, because by early 2006, the stock started moving up. By early February, it was at $23. The overall market made MacArthur uneasy, however, and because Polycom met his target of $22, he bailed out, garnering a 50 percent gain in six months. MacArthur remained convinced, however, that the videoconferencing industry would gain more believers and the stock would continue to go up over time. And it did, climbing to $32 by the end of 2006. On March 26, 2007, Polycom hit a high of $36.

Rewards of Concentration

Many active practitioners of the "Concentration" maxim continue to out-power the market. One of them is William Harnisch, chief executive and chief investment officer of Peconic Partners, a New York–based firm with assets under management of more than $1 billion. Part of the assets he manages comes from other money managers, including hedge funds. Harnisch regards diversification as the "plain vanilla of investing." To catch the "high waves and snare sizable gains, you need to concentrate your capital in sure winners," he asserts. Why diversify, he asks, when you can concentrate the money on just a few stocks that will excel? Harnisch argues that investors can as easily lose a big chunk of their capital investing in 100 stocks representing every industry. The idea should be to pick the best stock—no matter which industry it is in. Harnisch, who buys up to ten percent of the stock's shares outstanding, bases his stock picks on both fundamental and technical analyses. Although Harnisch is a long-term investor, he takes a proactive style of investing because, he says, "change is constant."

Investing in 100 stocks makes it impossible to know all of them well. In one of his letters to shareholders of his Berkshire Hathaway, where he is chairman and CEO, Warren Buffett used a rather amusing quote from Billy Rose, which drove home his point on diversification: "If you have a harem of forty women, you never get to know any of them very well."

Harnisch first focuses on a company's fundamentals, and then analyzes the stock's chart patterns over at least five years. The stock's technical behavior is as important to him as the fundamentals. Typically, his top ten ideas account for 40 to 50 percent of his fund's total investment. His largest concentration in a stock ranges from 5 to 10 percent of his portfolio.

"Our success is due to our constantly monitoring the market and our individual stock holdings so we can efficiently and quickly jump on the changing market conditions," says Harnisch. His proactive concentrated investment strategy has brought rich rewards. Since 1990, Harnisch's portfolio has produced a masterful 20 percent compounded returns annually.

How does Harnisch avoid great risks with concentrated positions in a limited number of stocks? "We make sure we control the risks," he says confidently. As much as he can, Harnisch visits companies and talks to the CEOs and other management officers. He also talks to major suppliers and the companies' top customers. He is particularly consummate in analyzing balance sheets, income statements, and other pertinent financial data. "That is the way to get an edge on each company we invest in, by getting to know as much as we can," says Harnisch.

Harnisch makes sure the companies he invests in are dominant in their businesses, with strong and transparent financials and a sustainable, attractive risk-reward profile. When a stock has a technical breakdown for whatever reason, he sends out an "alert-watch" to his staff for possible quick changes. But that doesn't alter his long-term approach. "We simply but urgently adjust our positions accordingly," he adds.

How does Harnisch come to a decision to get out of a stock? "On fundamentals, we get out when we no longer believe in the original investment thesis we had in the stock, or when our target price objective has been met," he says. But the long aspect of that, he explains, "is we continue to watch the stock, for a possible return to it—if the price or reason for our getting out of the stock is alleviated." On the technical side, "we bail out when a stock violates its 200-day moving average price trend, or when the stock hits a period of super-normal appreciation in its price," he says.

Peconic's business evolved from Fortsmann Leff Associates' asset management business, which Harnisch managed from the late 1970s. As the CEO and chief investment officer at Forstmann Leff, Harnisch managed more than $8 billion in assets. By December of 2004, he and several hedge fund managers separated from Forstmann to focus exclusively on Peconic Partners' hedge business, in which Harnisch has invested his own money, exceeding $100 million.

Let us look at an example of a stock where Peconic Partners used the strategy of concentration to full advantage.

Best Buy: Is It Ever!

Best Buy (BBY) is one of Harnisch's giant winners in his concentrated portfolio—and he still owns the stock as of this writing on November 19, 2007. Harnisch made his initial purchase in 1997. Best Buy has rewarded Harnisch well through all those years.

Best Buy is America's number-one retailer of consumer electronics products, including personal computers, software, video games, and other home entertainment products. With more than 1,100 stores in the U.S., Canada, and China, Best Buy is described by Standard & Poor's as the "best-of-class" U.S. consumer electronics retailer, based on its digital product focus, knowledgeable sales staff, and effective advertising and marketing campaigns. The company's sales focus on advanced TVs, laptops, and digital imaging products will continue to support double-digit revenue growth, says S&P in a report. Even as the average selling prices of digital TVs have declined, the drop should fire up sales volume and continue to drive Best Buy's growth.

Best Buy's stock has been a solid market performer in the sense that it invariably rebounds strongly after it stumbles. It has split its stock four times since 1998. As of November 19, 2007, the stock was at $46, down from its all-time high of $58 on April 6, 2006. But Harnisch was way ahead of everybody else in discovering Best Buy. He first bought shares in 1997, when it was selling at split-adjusted $1 a share. Yes, $1 a share. Harnisch continues to hold shares, although through Best Buy's highs and lows, he has traded in and out of the stock while holding enough shares to maintain the stock as a core holding in his long-term portfolio.

Harnish figured that as the largest retailer of consumer electronic products, Best Buy would grow rapidly because of the advent of digital TV. At that time, in 1997, digital TV was just coming out in the news and was not yet being mass-merchandised. Harnisch saw the magnitude of the potential for Best Buy: He calculated that the some 285 million households with television sets would eventually have to upgrade to digital when digital TV was rolled out. Sure enough, in 2006, Best Buy sold some 70 million sets of digital TVs. Best Buy still has a long way to go in catching up with demand from the remaining nondigital households and from the new households coming to the market.

So Harnisch "concentrated" in buying Best Buy shares, running up his total stake to 18 percent of Peconic's portfolio. Each year when the stock hit new highs, he would take some profits, but bought more shares when it tumbled significantly. Harnisch continued to hold on to the bulk of his stake even after the stock hit its all-time high of $58. He started feeling uneasy when the stock became widely held by investors. Yet the stock climbed to even higher highs.

Right about that time, the company started to change its strategy by reducing prices to compete with rivals like low-cost retailers Target and Wal-Mart, which were slowly attracting some of Best Buy's customers. The competition eroded Best Buy's profit margins, and by the fiscal third quarter (its fiscal year ends February 28) of 2006, Best Buy's earnings fell short of analysts' estimates. Harnisch was quick to move.

"I shorted the stock when it was at $45, while most everybody else was still bullish," says Harnisch. When the stock continued to slip, investors started getting nervous. Analysts began pulling down their earnings estimates in November and December of 2006. Then Harnisch saw something that convinced him to change his mind: At a company presentation to analysts in December that year, Harnisch heard an upbeat presentation, even though Best Buy's numbers were still off some analysts' estimates. He came out of the meeting convinced that Best Buy's inventories were coming down and that the company's plans for the next five years were impressive.

When Harnisch left that conference, his first call was to his trader: "Cover our short positions on Best Buy and buy more shares," he ordered forcefully. On February 21, 2007, Best Buy announced it was opening 130 new stores over the next year—90 in the U.S., 26 in China, and 14 in Canada. That announcement pushed the stock up. In the previous year, Best Buy had opened 90 new stores worldwide. In the meantime, the second largest electronics chain, Circuit City Stores, Inc., announced it was going to close 70 stores, most of them in Canada. As competitive as the retailing sector is, with all the discount stores led by Wal-Mart and the warehouse retail companies, such as Costco, milling around, Best Buy's stamina and durability in the business—consistently staying ahead of the pack—have been phenomenal.

At an average purchase cost of $1 a share, Harnisch is comfortable holding on to his equity stake in Best Buy. When the February

27, 2007 market crash hit, the stock dipped to $46.90. No matter. Harnisch expected the stock to resume its upward drive again, to at least $60. "When you get hold of something good like Best Buy, it pays to pay attention and continue holding it," he says. On December 31, 2007, Best Buy's stock closed at $52.65.

Don't Catch "Falling Knives"

Vincent Carrino, president of Brookhaven Capital Management, is also an avid and successful practitioner of the "Concentration" maxim. His actively managed portfolio is concentrated in just five to ten stocks at any given time. Although he screens about 100 stocks scouting for attractive long-term buys, Carrino focuses only on stocks he figures will double in price or go even higher.

In Carrino's experience, companies with such potential are usually the out-of-favor and ignored names on Wall Street. They're the "abandoned beauties," as he calls them. But be sure not to end up catching "falling knives," warns Carrino. He started his career at Citibank in 1980, working at its corporate finance department right after graduating from Stanford University's Business School that year. He was assigned to an area where merger and acquisition deals were hatched. From there, he joined Alliance Capital in 1983 as an airline and transportation analyst, where he also became involved in looking at companies that were likely takeover targets. He quit Alliance to form his own company, Brookhaven Capital Management, three years later.

Brookhaven manages Carrino's own money, plus some assets from a few mid-size institutional investment outfits. He also helps manage portfolios of several hedge funds. Since 1998, Carrino's portfolio has posted yearly compounded returns of 34 percent. In 2003 alone, his portfolio gained a heady 45 percent, topped by a stunning return of 63 percent in 2005. That wasn't even his best year, though. In 2006, he produced a staggering return of 88 percent. His basic principle is rooted in value investing, as opposed to Harnisch's focus on growth stocks. His universe is mostly the big-cap companies with strong franchises, good cash flow, and low-cost operations.

Carrino's big focus in on change—any change in a company or industry that portends to bring improvement in its value. Carrino is always on the lookout for some new twist that he believes will spur a change in the sales, earnings, or cash flow numbers. They could involve the movement of the dollar or the euro, or a change in interest rates.

"Such changes inevitably make the pendulum swing widely, between the lows and highs of the stock," notes Carrino.

He buys a stock when its "pendulum" swings to its lowest, and he sells when it is on its way to the top. Let us look at how this pendulum swinging produced winners for Carrino.

U.S. Steel: Definitely a Big Steal

One big home run for Carrino was U.S. Steel (X). He bought shares when nobody cared about the stock. In 2001, U.S. Steel was like a forgotten doormat. That was mainly because the steel industry was reeling from a capacity oversupply situation, with Japan the big supplier to the world's needs. But Carrino started to sense that demand for steel worldwide was starting to bulge, just after the American steel industry had severely cut back capacity.

Carrino believed that an uptick in demand after years of drought would benefit U.S. Steel. So he bought shares at about $12 a share in 2001, and he accumulated more shares until they ran up to 15 percent of his portfolio. That was how convinced he was that the price of steel would stage a comeback. By late 2002, it did. U.S. Steel's stock jumped, to $37. The company reported a swelling in global demand for its own products. Except for some occasional up-and-down blips along the way, industry fundamentals showed surprising strength, which eventually showed up in U.S. Steel's top and bottom lines.

The stock touched an all-time high of $93.90 on February 26, 2007. The following day, the market tumbled, and U.S. Steel dropped to $80 a share. Panic selling hit the stock. But guess what? By June 23, the stock vaulted to a 52-week high of $125.05. Any buyer who took advantage of the investor panic in February would have been well rewarded. With the subprime troubles erupting in the summer of 2007, the stock market went into another panic mode. But U.S. Steel was one of the few stocks that didn't collapse. On December 31, 2007, the stock stood firm at $120.91.

Because Carrino bought shares at around $12 a share, he did not feel like staying too long. He missed a big part of the stock's ascent to the upper $90s because he sold most of his shares when the stock was at $60 in 2006. Still, capturing a reward of about five times your capital is absolutely nothing to sneeze at. He was in it for the long term, but the generous returns over the short-term were too difficult to resist, even for a total concentrator. He was in the stock for about five years.

New Century Financial—an Early Catch

You have heard of the severe pain and heavy losses that investors and subprime mortgage lenders have suffered. But there were people who surmised early on that the subprime mortgage debacle was coming. One such investor who made a tidy bundle and moved on was Vincent Carrino. New Century Financial Co. (NEW), a mortgage banking company that provides subprime mortgage loans for single-family houses, got hammered in March 2007 because of the housing slump that hurt companies catering to mortgage borrowers with poor credit ratings. The stock lost some 84 percent of its value in four weeks between February and March 2007, plunging to as low as $3.50 a share as of March 9, 2007. But Carrino had been an early bird in the stock: He bought shares in 2000—before the stock rocketed to higher levels. Fortunately for him, he was able to read the handwriting on the wall in 2004, when he decided to jump out of the stock with hefty profits.

Carrino seized a great opportunity in New Century that, he says, reminded him of what he saw in U.S. Steel. He started buying shares of New Century in 2000 at an average cost of $10 a share, adjusted for splits. High interest rates hurt New Century at the time, which shook the stock. New Century's pendulum had swung to its lowest point by then, which caught Carrino's attention. He was convinced that the Federal Reserve Board would have to start cutting interest rates to help stimulate the soggy U.S. economy. The tragic terrorist attacks on September 11, 2001 underscored even more that need. A few months after the terrorist attacks, the Fed did reduce interest rates to make sure the economy didn't fall off into a recession.

The banks and financial institutions, including New Century, were jubilant. The drop in interest rates was manna from heaven. Before then, in 2000, the company was very much in the red, but that changed in 2001 when the Fed cut rates. New Century quickly went into the black and posted net income of $48 million. By 2004, New Century did even better, posting robust profits of $375.57 million. Predictably, that triggered a mad dash for the stock. The stock soared to a high of $66.95 a share. "I kept thinking it was déjà vu, à la U.S. Steel, all over again," recalled Carrino.

Was it time to bail out having been handed such a generous reward? The pendulum had swung up. So Carrino started reducing his stake, which, by then, was 25 percent of his portfolio. Having bought shares at such a rock-bottom price, Carrino finally decided in late 2004 to take all his money off the generous table and unloaded his entire New Century holdings. It was a timely move, because by 2005, the stock started to scale back, to $64.38, although the company still posted good earnings of $416 million, or $7.17 a share. By the end of 2005, things turned for the worse. The housing industry showed signs of weariness after so many years of robust activity, exacerbated—once again—by rising interest rates. The stock started heading south as the company took the brunt of the Fed's boost in interest rates, increased loan delinquencies, and the collapse in demand for housing. On February 28, 2007, a lawsuit was filed in the U.S. District Court for the Central District of California against the company, claiming that management during April 7, 2006 and February 7, 2007 issued misleading statements and concealed material adverse facts from the investing public.

The stock as of February 28 was at $15. Carrino was in the stock for about four years. It wasn't a short-term holding, but he knew when to get out. He made six times his capital. On March 8, the company announced that it was stopping extending home loans, deepening concern over the prospects of more mortgage defaults. With the company facing bankruptcy, its stocks fell to the $3 level.

AMR: Up High in the Sky

Vincent Carrino used the same high-low pendulum swings when he bought shares of AMR, parent of the world's largest airline, American Airlines, in 2005, at $8.50 a share. Nobody then wanted anything to do with the airlines, with traffic down to historically low levels and costs, including jet fuel, on the rise. Even now, many believe that airlines are the worst stocks to invest in. This is true, but only for those who don't know the industry well. Carrino has strong connections with the industry because he was once an airline analyst. Not only did he have good sources of information in the industry, he also knew how to decipher the many intricate factors affecting the economics of flying. The situation in 2004 was much different. The airline industry was soaring, and shares of AMR had rocketed to $40 on April 4, 2004, a time when airline stocks were among the high fliers.

But the following year, 2005, it was a different story for the airlines. The group dove some 25 percent early that year when the price of oil escalated just as passenger traffic started to dip, partly due to higher airfares. Once again, Carrino's interest was drawn to the airlines, as he sensed that something was changing—something that he thought would be a godsend to the airlines. The change he saw coming was a decline in oil prices from their lofty levels. Such a scenario, he believed, would definitely produce attractive profits for the better managed airlines, AMR in particular. Carrino felt at the time that the industry's woes were already much reflected in the depressed price of the airline stocks. So even a modest drop in oil prices, he figured, would send AMR's stock flying again. Carrino made his move and started accumulating AMR shares, at $8.50 a share.

By late 2005, AMR shares started taking off, reaching $24 by the end of the year. Carrino held on to his shares, which had grown to about 15 percent of his portfolio. Oil prices did come down from nearly $80 a barrel to $70, and by mid-2006, they came down even more, to $52, but only to rise again in a flip-flop fashion to the $60 to $61 a barrel level.

It didn't matter, because on January 19, 2007, AMR's stock flew to a high of $40.66, largely because of the combination of the drop in oil prices, heavy passenger traffic, and fare hikes. AMR's earnings made a sharp turnaround, from a loss of $5.21 a share in 2005 to profits of 98 cents in 2006. Revenues jumped from $18.6 billion to $22.5 billion. Obviously, Carrino had been perfectly justified in zeroing in on AMR at the time that he did.

Business was extraordinarily good, and the numbers so impressive, that speculation swirled in mid-February 2007 that AMR was being pursued by private equity groups, which sources said included Goldman Sachs and British Airways. Apparently, some people heard from industry sources that representatives of the private equity groups had informally talked with AMR about a plan to propose some kind of a deal. But AMR declined to say anything about it. And Goldman Sachs threw cold water on the subject by not only declining to comment, but also giving out off-the-record comments to journalists and analysts that "nothing was going on."

Maybe. But if you were talking privately with a target company, you would not say anything publicly either. The usual strategy is to keep silent. But if you were Goldman Sachs, whose interests ran the gamut—from brokerage, proprietary stock trading to investment banking and merger-and-acquisition deals, plus a hedge fund armed with billions of dollars—wouldn't you just want everybody to shut up?

If a deal came out, then Goldman Sachs or AMR would open up. But not until then, because it would jeopardize negotiations. The sources for the story made it a point to insist that nothing was definite about the deal and it was possible nothing would come out of it. AMR's stock was trading then (on February 9) at about $36. On February 26, 2007—the day before the February 27, 2007, market meltdown—AMR closed at $36.37 a share. By March 8, 2007, the stock closed at $33.30. Carrino finally bailed out of the stock at about that price. He made more than three times his original investment in more than two years. It was another timely exit. By September 11, 2007, the stock was at $24.

When I wrote about the speculation in my "Inside Wall Street" column in the *BusinessWeek* issue dated February 26, 2007 (the magazine reaches subscribers ten days before the issue date), some analysts said they thought such a deal was logical. Many deals that have been hatched and completed were illogical to start with. With so many private equity groups stuffed with billions of dollars to invest and not too many prospective targets around, logic, like beauty, is very much in the eye of the beholder. Improving fundamentals in the airline business, and at AMR in particular, drove up the stock. The industry was in a consolidation mode then, and it still is. AMR will be one of those that will be looked at as a possible acquisition target. Already it is considered a target by some airline experts.

The speculation about AMR and British Airways (BAB) getting together might yet develop legs. On March 9, 2007, AMR Chairman and CEO Gerard Arpey commented on the impact of a proposed "Open Skies" agreement that would open London's Heathrow Airport to other airlines. American is one of only two carriers permitted to fly from the U.S. to Heathrow, Europe's largest airport. Speaking at American's annual conference call with analysts, Arpey said American Airlines would suffer from increased competition under the proposed Open Skies agreement. But he argued that the "blow would be softened if the two airlines (AMR and British Airways) got some antitrust immunity, as some competitors have, to combine some of their business operations."

Apparently, the speculation that the two carriers were talking about a merger deal stemmed from conjecture that an Open Skies policy would be detrimental to both of them and that one way to avert that was a merger. So, a deal in some form or another might still happen. In 2007, when oil prices started resurging and touched the $100-a-barrel level, airline stocks plummeted, including AMR's, which dropped to $14.03 on December 31, 2007.

Northwest Airlines: Still Northbound

AMR was a terrific home run for Carrino, but he bagged an even larger prize in Northwest Airlines, which had expected to emerge from bankruptcy in June 2007. Carrino bought shares in 2005, weeks after Northwest filed for Chapter 11 protection on September 14, 2005, when the stock was selling at 40 cents a share. That wasn't a typographical error. Yes, the stock was trading at 40 cents when Carrino dared to buy shares.

Again, Carrino concentrated a lot of money in the stock, although the company was in dire financial straits. He ended up buying a five percent stake in the friendless airline, which was the number-five

U.S. carrier. What attracted Carrino to what looked like a risky stock? Northwest fell right into the core of his strategy: With his purchase cost at 40 cents a share, he figured Northwest was attractive, considering that it was still a major U.S. airline and its pendulum was at its low point.

Using his experience as a former airline industry analyst, Carrino figured Northwest was far from dead and that it would rise again—if it were not bought out first by another airline before it emerged from bankruptcy. The numbers looked good to Carrino. Even when it was in bankruptcy, Northwest in 2005 posted sales of $12.3 billion, versus 2004's $11.2 billion. In 2006, sales totaled $12.6 billion. Carrino liked the fact that the Chapter 11 filing helped eliminate most of the airline's problems, primarily the mounting labor costs associated with pilots and other union employees.

The industry was consolidating, and Northwest was certainly buy-out bait, in Carrino's opinion. He based his opinion on the surprise bid by US Airways on October 15, 2006 to buy Delta Air Lines, which was also in bankruptcy. US Airways later withdrew its $9.7 billion bid on January 31, 2007, after Delta's management and its employees showed open hostility to it. Delta came out of bankruptcy in early 2007.

In the third quarter of 2006, Northwest posted operating profits of $272 million on sales of $3.4 billion. Due to its bankruptcy, the airline had charges of $1.4 billion. Those results included gains from lower labor costs. The airline cut annual expenses by $2.5 billion. For all of 2006, Northwest reported operating earnings of $763 million, or $3 a share.

I wrote a story on the speculation that Northwest was a possible takeover target in the *BusinessWeek* issue of November 27, 2006. The stock by then had soared from 40 cents a share on July 7, 2006 to $1.75 on November 15, 2007. Carrino estimated that, based on the numbers put out by Northwest, the airline would post a "dramatic upswing" in 2007 operating earnings, to between $500 million and $1 billion.

His estimate was on target because, for all of 2006, Northwest already posted operating earnings of $763 million. By December 13, 2006, the stock soared to $6.55 a share, a dramatic upswing, indeed, from 40 cents when Carrino bought in. Carrino acknowledged that he could not help but sell his equity position at that high point. He had achieved his target in the stock way ahead of expectations. In all, Carrino held the stock for more than two years. Northwest emerged from Chapter 11 protection in the second quarter of 2007. On December 31, 2007, Northwest's stock closed at $14.51.

The essence of the "Concentrate" commandment is to make sure an investor doesn't dilute his or her portfolio with so many assorted types of stocks. A few good ones are better at producing big returns for your portfolio than 100 so-so stocks. Certainly, concentration goes to the heart of stock picking: Investors need not be distracted by many strategic choices. When you come upon a good stock, multiply your rewards by investing more money in it.

In this chapter, I advised you that when you embark on investing in the stock market, you should focus on a strategy that is logical. Don't fall for the popular strategies like diversification. What is popular in the stock market is not necessarily bulletproof. As an example, most investors love to go after stocks that are widely popular, high-flying stocks. They chase after the stocks that are the present choice of the crowd. They go for the winners.

In the next chapter, I advise you not to go after winners if you want to pick the new batch of mega-winners. Entitled "Buy the Losers," I suggest that the winners circle is the last place to find the future champions of the stock market. I discuss the folly of chasing after stocks that have had their day in the sun, with a big run-up, and advocate buying the "losers" that have the potential of ending up as big winners.

COMMANDMENT 3

Buy the Losers

"The worse a situation becomes, the less it takes to turn it around—and the bigger the upside."

—George Soros

The Buy the Losers commandment isn't easy to obey. It goes against the grain because we are used to cheering the winner and showing only sympathy for the loser.

How does buying the losers equate to winning in the stock market? We will demonstrate that betting on the losers is the smarter way to get to the winner's circle. It is true that everybody loves a winner. This is especially true in the stock market. To imply to friends that you are a market cognoscenti, you would nonchalantly remark that you just bought the fast-rising shares of Google, rather than mention buying a stock that is down, like Citigroup when it was on the ropes (because of the subprime mortgage crisis), or the underdog Pfizer, which has been investor ignored.

To be frank, buying stocks when they are skyrocketing is far riskier than buying Citigroup or Pfizer when it hit five-year lows. Buying the stock du jour isn't the intelligent way to play the stock market. Unless you bought at the absolute bottom, much of the big money has already been made in that stock. True, a stock like the streaking Google might be one of the few exceptions and could well continue marching upward as it breaks new ground in new products and services. In fact, Google on November 5, 2007 announced that it was developing software for mobile phones, which would include search capabilities that would enable wireless carriers to attract more customers. And Google also may end up winning a wireless spectrum at the U.S. Federal Communications Commission auction. With a wireless spectrum, Google might decide to become a national mobile carrier, as well. Those two factors could well propel Google to higher ground and push its stock price higher. With such added potential, Google would, indeed, be an exception.

More often than not, however, you end up in the losers' corner if you pursue the market stars when they are skyrocketing. The best strategy would be to find the next Google, or another stock whose growth potential is similar to that of the Web search giant, and is selling at a modest price.

To achieve that goal, we advise investors to buy shares of the "losers," instead, for reasons we enumerate in this chapter. However, it takes a major reconditioning of the mind to adopt the Buy the Losers maxim. It takes a lot of rethinking and an uncommon but refreshing mind-set to look at the stock market for what it really is and what most investors ignore: a market of opportunity.

Winners Disguised as Losers

In the same way that we encouraged investors in the first chapter to adopt a panic-free mind-set, we advocate a strategy of buying the "losers"—for investors to find the next batch of winners. We really mean buying the losers that have the potential for bouncing back as winners. How do you distinguish a downright loser from one that is a loser with strong prospects of turning around—a winner presently disguised as a loser? This chapter discusses how and cites examples.

It isn't surprising that investors tend to pay more attention to stocks that are in the fast lane, and unhesitatingly chase them. When investors look at the financial pages in newspapers or the Internet, their first inclination is to look at the list of big year-to-date percentage gainers. But what's wrong is they also scan the winners' list to find more stocks to add to their portfolios. The common perception is that buying the winners enhances their chances of beating the market.

The winners' column is the *last* place to look for future megawinners. The stocks in the winners' corner have made the grade. Except for some that might have special reasons to help them continue doing well, the rest of those winners are likely to meander and later switch to the slow lane. These are the stocks the institutions are likely to dump sooner than you think. In all likelihood, these were the same stocks they had purchased much earlier and then dumped after making money on them.

The institutional investors—asset managers at banks, investment houses, mutual funds, pension funds, hedge funds, and the like—unload stocks for a variety of reasons, some of them based on fundamentals. In many cases, however, they sell for reasons that are part of a particular strategy that has nothing to do with a company's value. Profit taking is the common reason behind the selling.

Although the institutions proclaim to be long-term investors, these investors with billions of dollars to play with are among the heavy short-term traders and pretty much behave like short-term flippers when opportunity knocks. Institutional players need to do trades for short-term gains because, for every quarter, they have to show profits on stocks they bought for clients. In the process, the idea of long-term investing is sacrificed so they can display consistently high quarterly total returns. Besides, they also need a big cash stash on the side to be able act swiftly on any new enticing stock that comes along. Obviously, there are other reasons why they sell.

Earnings disappointments spark selling. Or, in the case of Big Pharma or the biotechs, the Food and Drug Administration might have signaled a negative reaction to a new drug. These are enough to trigger selling by investors even before they check the facts. In such cases, the big investors are quick to bail out and then buy the same stocks later when they go down to much lower prices. It is at that point that these institutions play the Buy the Losers strategy. So why shouldn't individual investors adopt the same strategy right at the outset?

The place to find potential winners is the usually ignored and unlikeliest place—the losers' list. In my experience, what seems "obvious" in the stock market isn't always the real story. Often there is a story behind a story. For instance, a company's failure to meet analysts' earnings expectations might just be an aberration and could provide the opportunity to buy a fallen stock on the cheap. There are risks, but if you are right, the rewards are worth it.

The ultimate question is how an investor can determine whether a particular "loser" can morph into a winner. One answer is "due-diligence" research, which is a top priority for any investor. You must be up on the news about the market and acquire significant knowledge about stocks in general. When you hear or read that a stock suddenly plunged and has caused a stir, the first thing to do is read up as much as you can about the company to find out what caused the heavy selling. The business press and online blogs and chat rooms will be busy with stories about a stock under fire, particularly if they involve high-profile companies.

In most cases, investors overreact to bad news, which prompts instant selling.

The selling could quickly result in a stock dropping 5 percent or more. If you look behind the factors involved, you might find that analysts' overreaction fueled the selling. They can be as guilty in driving a stock down as the panicky investors. Analysts for the most part make sure they protect themselves by quickly recommending the sale of a stock first and asking questions later. It is a form of protection, but in fact they should have gotten wind of the problem ahead of everybody else and alerted their clients. When analysts realize they got it wrong, they just write a report revising their call. In the meantime, they already have stirred concern, if not panic, among investors.

Against such a backdrop, the Buy the Losers maxim is a logical rule to adopt. However, for investors who are not yet acquainted with the market, the stocks more suited under this maxim are the large-cap stocks. Information is widely available on large-cap stocks, and it takes little effort to check on them.

Watch the High-Profile Stocks

An investor can keep tabs on these large caps because they are more widely traded. They are also the favorites of institutional investors because of their liquidity and ease of trading. But it is worth repeating that primary research is needed to be adequately informed and be ahead of the game. If a company like Wal-Mart, for instance, suddenly drops 2 or 3 percent in a day, there would be ample media coverage about it. That helps investors decide whether they want to bail out, short the stock, or buy shares. It helps when the company involved is a high-profile company. Similar to what was recommended in Chapter 1, "Buy Panic," the large-cap, high-profile companies are the ones to choose from in scouting for future winners.

In fact, one such widely popular stock, Apple, represented a good example of what we are talking about. Apple's stock price dropped some 2 percent to 3 percent within a few days after the company announced in August that it was cutting the price of its latest product, iPhone, by some 30 percent. That caused a big ruckus among Apple fans, who purchased the revolutionary phone weeks before the surprise price cut. When the complaints hit the headlines, some analysts were quick to downgrade Apple's stock. They figured that Apple's sales would suffer from the price reductions. And they also surmised that sales must be slowing down overall. Otherwise, why would Apple cut the price?

Apple's stock dropped instantly. As it turned out, however, sales of iPhone continued to jump—exceeding analysts' expectations. To make amends with its distraught customers, Apple awarded refunds to make up the price difference. Predictably, Apple's stock price surged, from about $117 in August to a new high of $153 on September 27, 2007. Investors who spotted Apple's presence among the losers on August 16, 2007, when it fell to $117 a share from $127 two days before and purchased shares, would have made an easy $10 a share in those three days alone. Had the investors held on to Apple's stock for a longer period, their profits would have been even more flavorful. As of December 28, 2007, the stock hit an all-time high of $199.83. What a winner for a supposed "loser"!

In some cases, the severity of a group's decline is quite ominous. A case in point was the collapse in mid-2007 of homebuilders' stocks due to the housing slump that was exacerbated by the crisis that gripped the subprime mortgage lenders. The drop in home sales and the genesis of the subprime mortgage woes started in 2006. By the summer of 2007, the deterioration in housing sales intensified, worsened by the bankruptcy filings by some companies in the subprime mortgage business. By mid-December of 2007, the stock prices of most homebuilders had plunged by 30 percent to 77 percent for the year.

Homebuilding executives predicted then that a recovery might not happen until 2009. The housing debacle is an example of why investors have to keep on top of events that could impact their portfolios—or stocks they might want to buy.

Were there any housing stocks that would have been candidates under the Buy the Losers rule? Most definitely there were. Many of the depressed homebuilders stocks were perfect candidates to buy not only under the Buy the Losers maxim but also under the Buy Panic commandment in the first chapter. But the housing stocks that appeared to be more inclined to recover fast from the crisis had to be held for the long haul, because as some chief executives of companies in the business have said publicly, it might take a year or two before things get better.

If you had applied the Buy the Losers maxim, you would have already decided which housing companies you would want to own when the group started being hit. And you would have to expect that the price of those stocks could go down even more. But waiting to catch the bottom of the market or any individual stock is never a workable strategy. If a stock has gone down by 50 percent in price, it is likely that any further decline would not be another 50 percent. A drop of another 5 percent to 10 percent is more likely. But the important issue at this point was to determine which of the stocks could best withstand further erosion in value. Again, research and homework would come in handy.

Part of the problem for bargain hunters was the continued negative media coverage that the housing industry was getting, which surely was one of the reasons why housing stock prices kept spiraling down. For sure, housing stocks would continue to be volatile. The wreckage has been severe for the banks holding mortgage loans, particularly mortgages to people with poor credit risks, and for the homebuilders and other industries that depend heavily on the housing industry for their business.

But it would have been logical to expect that after such a deep decline, the next big move for the housing stocks would be on the upside, based on the history of the group's past performance when they were clobbered by similar misfortunes in the past. In 1999, a similar bust knocked the industry, and it took about three years for the group to recover. Stock prices declined an average of 50 percent.

The 2007 housing crisis had already exceeded that point by November of 2007. So at that particular point in time, the opportunity to start bargain hunting among housing stocks was close at hand.

Homebuilders: Ripe for the Picking

By year-end 2007, I figured some of the stocks had become too oversold, and quite ripe to buy for investors looking for the "losers" that would eventually morph into big winners. I would have placed my bets on three homebuilders stocks: Toll Brothers (TOL), which hit a low of $19.57 on September 26, 2007, versus its high of $35.35 on February, 2, 2007; Centex (CTX), which was knocked down to a low of $21.66 on November 8, 2007, compared to its high of $57.84 on December 6, 2006; and KB Home (KBH), another that was clobbered to a low of $24.09 on September 26, 2007, versus a high of $55 on February 2, 2007. On December 28, 2007, Toll closed at $20.06 a share, Centex at $24.97, and KB Home at $21.08.

These are all large-cap stocks, and they're the more high-profile housing stocks that trade on the New York Stock Exchange. They are good candidates for long-term holdings in what obviously has been a depressed corner of the stock market. Analysts continued cutting their sales and earnings forecasts, as well as their stock price targets.

By the end of October 2007, Standard & Poor's housing analyst Kenneth M. Leon, who recommended buying shares of Toll, a builder of upscale homes, in a November 10, 2007 report, expected the company's sales for all of 2007 to drop by 22 percent, and gross margins by 14 percent. For 2008, he forecast the erosion in sales to abate and drop by only 3 percent, and gross margins to recover by the second half of 2008. Centex, a major homebuilder that sells homes in 25 states, is also in home mortgage banking and title insurance. The sales volume trend at Centex showed a slower deterioration than some of its peers. KB Home, a diversified homebuilder with operations in the largest U.S. markets, is one of the five largest single-family home builders. Its exposure to entry-level buyers remained KB's biggest risk, but it had reduced debt and continues to generate free cash flow.

UBS investment bank's analyst David Goldberg, who recommended buying the stock in a September 28, 2007 report, noted that KB's debt-to-capital ratio was among the lowest in the housing group, and it had cash of $646 million, which gave it flexibility to take advantage of opportunities.

These stocks are great examples of how to pick stocks off their lows. It is possible that in the ensuing weeks the stocks could have gotten pummeled some more, but buying them at such huge discounts to their average price can't steer you to the poor house. The housing stocks made it quite elementary: The industry was in a slump, and all the homebuilders stocks were highly depressed. It was relatively easy to cherry-pick stocks. Because the homebuilders were in the same level of trouble, the only factors to consider were which of them had sufficient cash and asset resources to withstand the massive drop in property prices, which stock had fallen off its historical price-earnings ratios and by how much, which stock had the bigger percentage declines, and which among the stocks had a history of bouncing back from similar problems in the past. You can get most if not all of this data from Yahoo.com, Value Line, or S&P. Simply reading the newspapers or magazines and reading other online reports on housing stocks would provide some answers to these basic questions.

So, in the final analysis, how should investors go about picking the right stock from the "loser's" lair for potential winners? Start by checking the stock's high and low price range for at least the past 52 weeks. It is a positive sign when a stock is selling at or near its 52-week low. Most stocks in the winners circle trade near their 52-week highs. That in itself is a negative when looking for potential winners. When a stock is perched high on a pedestal, the next move in most cases is down, down to possibly steeper lows. But when a stock is coming off its bottom, or somewhere close to its low, that often indicates that it may be poised to move to higher ground.

Needless to say, research is extremely important—and even more so when you are trying to check into troubled smaller-capitalization stocks, which trade mostly on the NASDAQ and American Stock Exchange. The small- and mid-cap stocks require extra digging, because the amount of public information about them is limited. The market's appetite for stocks with valuations below $500 million is not as large or efficient as those for the big-caps, precisely because of the shortage of information and a low market capitalization, which turn off Wall Street analysts.

As we discussed in the first chapter, one of the best places to get information is from the company. Companies are always glad to send their annual reports and other information to investors. Most of them have investor relations officers who handle communications with investors. And there is the magic of the Internet, which has changed the dynamics of investing. All kinds of information are available by just logging on to a company's Web site, or through online destinations such as Google, Yahoo.com, AOL.com, or any newspaper and news magazines, which are also available online.

The fact that relatively fewer people know a lot about small- or mid-cap stocks (compared to large caps) can be an advantage. The element of surprise is one twist that benefits a small company. When a relatively obscure company or one of the "losers" surprises investors with positive news about earnings or a product, you can bet the stock will jump more than a large-cap company would under similar circumstances.

A company with shares outstanding of just 100 million to 500 million is definitely bound to react more sharply to good news than, say, IBM, which has 1.5 billion shares outstanding, or Microsoft, with 9.8 billion shares. It takes few shares to jog or nudge a small-cap stock. So when positive news hits, the small-caps react faster and more sharply. However, the Microsofts of the world, with vast numbers of shares outstanding, are like battleships in the ocean. They can only turn slowly to change directions. However, the good news is that they're also more immune to bad news than the small fries are. The conclusion on this issue is that regardless of size—large-cap or small-cap— a portfolio's strength ultimately depends on the quality of the stocks in it.

Outside of the housing stocks, one stock that some investors who abide by the Buy the Losers maxim targeted is US Airways, one of the major airlines that came out of bankruptcy in 2006. After emerging from bankruptcy, the stock climbed as high as $63 on November 11, 2006. From that high point, the airline started to descend, touching down to $21 by November 9, 2007. That's a drop of more than 60 percent. It's a steep discount relative to its peers, which dropped much less, to about 20 percent to 30 percent. So, compared to its major competitors, US Airways suffered the most. By November 16, 2007, the stock had inched up to $23. Already it was starting to bounce up, albeit slowly. But that price of $21 to $23 provided a propitious buying point, because all the reasons behind the drop had already been factored into the stock's price. What were the factors behind the decline? The rocketing price of crude oil, for one, was a major blow. Operational and labor problems that remained unresolved, partly because of US Airways' recent merger with America West Airlines, were also a negative. And the volatile stock market affected the airlines. For a long while in 2007, there was talk of a recession looming.

Another factor that the bargain hunters looked at was the earnings forecasts by analysts. Goldman Sachs and Morgan Stanley, who turned bullish and rated US Airways stock a buy in October 2007 when the airline was trading at lower levels, expected the airline to earn $5.75 a share for 2007, up from 2006's $5.44. US Airways was making money, yet its stock was diving. That is a bullish sign. So, given those factors alone, US Airways represented a buy-on-its low type of a stock. The good news ahead for US Airways is that the price of oil, which soared to nearly $100 a barrel for several days in November 2007, cannot possibly stay at those high levels for long. The capacity cuts by the other airlines were also positive for US Airways, because it gave the airline the chance to raise fares as demand outstripped capacity. Also, the integration problems involving the America West merger were being resolved faster than many expected.

The Price Earnings Ratio Puzzle

A stock's price-earnings ratio, or p/e, is another benchmark that investors need to look at in evaluating a stock. That's the price of a stock divided by its per-share earnings. A common perception among investors is that a high p/e proclaims success. To some, that indicates the stock deserves to be bought. We disagree. Although it may be true that a high p/e ratio suggests the company has done well, investors looking for the next big winner should not be tempted by it.

A high p/e more often than not is a signal that the stock might have already fully run its upward course. It is possible that the stock might still have some fuel for it to run up some more, but it would be more realistic to assume that it might be ready to run out of gas. Of course, there are exceptions. Some stocks like Google trade at steep p/e multiples and continue to go up. But we are talking about finding future winners. With a stock that is trading at the high of its usual p/e pattern, the stock has little room for error and may not be able to withstand unfavorable news.

On the other hand, a stock with a low p/e multiple has a lot going for it. The upside is wide open. It suggests that the p/e ratio has enough room to advance on any piece of upbeat news. More often than not, a stock trading at a low multiple indicates that most of the bad news is already reflected in the stock. Expectations are already low, so when the stock gets positive news, it would be a welcome event that would drive up the stock—fast.

You can obtain data and charts about a stock's trading pattern from a number of sources, including stock reports from Standard & Poor's Corp., Value Line Publishing Inc., Barron's, or Investors Business Daily. Among newswire services, Bloomberg, a widely popular online news and information service, is an important source, along with close competitor Reuters. Thompson First Call, a subscription-based investor information service, also provides an array of information about stocks and their performance.

S&P publishes a synopsis on each stock, mainly those included in its various stock indexes. They are concise and a convenient source of information and data. Each report displays a chart of the stock, a summary of what the company does, and the company's recent activities, including revenue and earnings updates. Stock brokers, who have access to them, usually share such information with their clients. Again, stockbrokers and financial advisors are subscribers to such publications and receive reports like what the S&P or Value Line publishes.

Bloomberg's service, which most brokerage houses use, provides a much more comprehensive report on companies than the other sources because it updates its information daily. It shows how a stock is behaving "live" based on current-event coverage like a newswire does. In like manner, Reuters provides news coverage as well as inclusive data on stocks and companies that are essential to catching the latest information. Reuters also provides a service in which it reviews and analyzes various companies and their stocks.

Value Line publishes a weekly *Investment Survey* that analyzes each stock, accompanied by data on trading and company perform-ance. Like the S&P, Value Line rates the stocks based on its own ranking and valuation benchmarks. In its weekly reports, Value Line shows the trading range of a stock for at least the past ten years. From there, you get a pretty good idea of where the stock is and what its "batting" average is. A stock's high and low points monthly indicate how solid a stock is—or is not.

Some of the big-cap stocks that we examine in this chapter were ideal candidates for the Buy the Losers commandment. They turned off investors when they got into some trouble. Most analysts who tracked them had little hope that they would ever recover. But they did. These "losers" became outright winners.

These large-cap stock winners are Research in Motion, which trades on the NASDAQ with the ticker symbol RIMM; Time Warner, which trades on the New York Stock Exchange with the symbol TWX; and Merck, another Big Board listed stock trading with the symbol MRK.

RIMM: A Stock in Motion

Research in Motion (RIMM) was a typical "fallen angel" whose stock picked up smartly from its lows. The company is best known as the maker of the popular BlackBerry, a wireless e-mail device. Its stock came under siege several times, which provided ample chances for investors to buy its stock at fire-sale prices. Each time it stumbled, the stock bounced back up. This happened at least three times since it started trading in 1999 at split-adjusted $1 a share. By November 17, 2007, the stock hit an all-time high of $133.03. Let's look at how RIMM prevailed over the many challenges it has conquered.

Investors who bought shares of RIMM in 1999 when the stock was selling at just $1 would have made a bundle, because from there the stock catapulted to $10 by the end of that year. But that was just the beginning of the stock's upswings and downswings, which really provided ample chances for the Buy the Losers investors to make money.

The entire stock market was on fire in 1999 and early 2000. But, to RIMM's credit, it had a great product—similar to the iPod—which wowed the market after its market introduction. The BlackBerry fever was on its way to climbing to great heights. But often, success gets sidetracked. By late 2000, the stock market started getting edgy, as investors morphed into acrophobes. The stock market had been on a tear, at full speed, powered by the rising popularity of the Internet and technology stocks. It was, in the words of then Fed Chairman Alan Greenspan, a case of "irrational exuberance" on the part of mindless investors. The market's heady bullishness did pause, as Greenspan's Fed machine tried to end the party by continuing to raise interest rates.

And so, the market collapse that Greenspan had wished for happened. The market tumbled to new depths by 2001. Shares of RIMM cascaded down to about $2. It was another golden opportunity to buy the stock, again at a bargain. True enough, the stock rallied shortly thereafter. But there was a significant development, although at the time that the stock popped to 6, nobody was paying much attention because of the turbulence in the market.

An unlikely turn of events occurred: In 2002, a lawsuit was filed against RIMM for patent infringement. The suit was filed by NTP Inc., one of the companies that accumulate patents in the hope of tripping up some company that might find itself using one of them in a particular product. NTP claimed that the BlackBerry was based on a patent RIMM didn't own. The lawsuit and the market's miserable trip south pulled RIMM 's stock back down to $2 by mid-2002.

For the Buy Panic adherents, that huge loss was manna from heaven: How many times do you see a stock with an exciting product and a management determined to push ahead aggressively provide so many tempting buying opportunities? Without fanfare, the stock once again showed its mettle by zooming up the following year, 2003, to $11. By 2004, the stock had rocketed to $34, a record high for the stock at the time. It seemed fair to expect that with such a fast run-up, RIMM deserved to rest and digest the fruit of its labor. In 2005, the stock did not do much; it meandered between $17 and $28—until wonderful news bobbed up. Sales boomed amid rising demand. Again, the stock pushed higher, to $47 in early 2006.

At around this time, however, the NTP lawsuit started getting heavy media coverage, and the stock once again suffered some downdraft. Rumors swirled that U.S. District Judge James R. Spencer might favor NTP's demand that RIMM halt its entire BlackBerry production. The judge had given NTP and RIMM ample opportunities to settle the case, but both were adamant and couldn't agree. NTP's demand that RIMM pay $160 million to settle had, by this time, escalated to a higher price: nearly $1 billion. Wall Street worried that NTP and RIMM might get locked in a corner. The stock dropped to $20.

It was about this time that I wrote a piece in my "Inside Wall Street" column about how some investors close to the matter were betting that an out-of-court settlement was brewing. Investors, in fact, had caught a scent of such a possibility, causing the stock to become active again—jumping from $20 to $30 on the rumors.

As I had anticipated, by March—just over a week after my story came out—RIMM and NTP agreed to settle, with the maker of BlackBerry paying $612.5 million. The stock blasted off to a 52-week high of $47 a share. Predictably, after such a fiery ascent, loads of profit-taking swept the stock. But to RIMM's credit, the stock withstood the heavy selling pressure.

At that point, the bears multiplied. Some analysts hoisted a sell recommendation in early January. The worry was that RIMM's growth would slow and profit margins would become lower, exacerbated by growing competition.

Unless RIMM's current expansion plans miscarry in a big way, I doubt that it will backtrack from where it has been. From the way the company has achieved its growth objectives—and from the stock's solid behavior—it should go to higher levels from here, to another record high.

The entry of Apple into the picture threw a curve ball to many analysts and investors. In June 2007, Apple, Inc. introduced iPhone, a revolutionary device that combines a smart phone with the iPod, capable of sending and receiving e-mails and allowing Internet browsing enhanced by a soft-touch keyboard and a camera. The happy users of Apple's widely popular music player, iPod, are expected to upgrade to iPhone, which is priced higher than the iPods, at $499. Two months after iPhone came out, Apple dropped the price to $399.

Some people worried that iPhone would eat into BlackBerry's vast turf. When Apple CEO Steve Jobs introduced the iPhone at the MacWorld Conference in January 2007, RIMM's stock tumbled about 10 percent from its closing price of $47 on January 8, the day before Apple's iPhone announcement.

But RIMM didn't show much concern. It has a lot of things going for it, including its own smart phones, Pearl and Curve, which are slim models designed mainly for the consumer market, with camera and music player functions. RIMM's vast market for the Black-Berry is the corporate customer, which represents about 92 percent of revenues.

By November 7, 2007, RIMM stock rocketed to an all-time high of $133.03 before dropping to $113.71 on December 31, 2007. On January 7, 2008, the stock dropped further, to $99.83. At that price, the stock once again looked like a good buy.

Apart from RIMM's plans to expand that market to foreign countries, the company has widened its reach to serve the consumer market. For fiscal year ending February 2008, Value Line projects an 80 percent revenue growth, to $5.5 billion, rising to $7.5 billion the following year.

The bottom line: There is still room for RIMM to grow—both in the U.S. and worldwide—in both consumer and enterprise (corporate) markets. New product launches will target both markets. Indeed, BlackBerry is still in the early stages of adoption in Asia and Latin America, which are huge areas of growth.

In November 2006, U.S. sales totaled 875,007 units compared with 220,796 units in November 2005, according to market researcher NPD Group. In the second quarter of 2007, RIMM announced it had shipped 2.4 million devices. That could bring total shipments for the entire year to 8 million units. Analysts forecast RIMM will earn $1.1 billion in the fiscal year ending February 2008 and $1.5 billion in fiscal 2009, up from fiscal 2007's $631.6 million. RIMM "remains top ranked for performance in the year ahead," says Value Line's Lester Ratcliff in an analysis on September 14, 2007.

Time Warner: The Giant Has Awakened

Time Warner, Inc. (TWX) was clearly a Buy the Loser type of stock. For years, it languished in the stock market's cellar. The giant media and entertainment conglomerate was quite a regular visitor to the list of Big Board's percentage losers.

It wasn't until November 2006 that Time Warner finally started to gain some upward traction, breaking out of the range of $18 to $20 a share, where it had been stuck since 2003. And on January 8, 2007, Time Warner crept up to a 52-week high of $23. That looks like a pittance of an advance. But the significant fact was that the stock, at long last, showed some upward momentum for the first time in five years. And it looks like it will continue to move up, mainly because of the changing attitude and scenario inside the company.

But for people who got into Time Warner stock in 1999 at a much higher price level—before Time Warner merged with America Online in January 2001 (when the stock flew to as high as $96 adjusted for three 2-for-1 stock splits)—the hike to $23 hardly matters. But in 2007, with the stock market buffeted by the subprime meltdown, Time Warner's stock was hit by yet another blow. The stock fell to $16.65 on December 28, 2007. Clearly the stock was again at its nadir, positioning it as an even better play in the Buy the Losers category.

Once upon a time, Time Warner's stock was an icon. In 1998, the stock traveled from $5.20 to $40 a share and then vaulted to $96 the following year. That was the peak, and the stock drifted down from there to $82. It started dropping some more, to as low as $32 as word got around that America Online, which was then one hot Internet stock, and Time Warner were contemplating a merger.

That merger happened on January 2001 in a $106 billion transaction, and it quickly became labeled as one of the worst deals ever, if not the worst. The stock continued to fall, down to $27 in the latter part of that year. By 2002, it had collapsed to $8 a share.

Those were the dark years for the once high-flying Time Warner empire. It was then that the stock, given up for dead by most investors, started showing up in the roster of big percentage losers. That, precisely, was the time to get on board. Looking back, it was the perfect opportunity to buy Time Warner for investors who had the foresight to adhere to the strategy of Buy the Losers.

Indeed, Time Warner was in the bargain box for a long time, and nobody paid it much attention. But some savvy money managers did accumulate shares at around $9 to $10 a share that year. Those who have held on surely made a killing, a tidy fortune.

One of them was Cynthia Ekberg Tsai, who is currently a principal of a $50 million investment fund called The Madelin Fund L.P. Cynthia bought Time Warner shares at around $10 a share, and held it. She has had ample experience on Wall Street, first as a broker for 16 years and then as an investor and venture capitalist on her own, after her divorce in 1995 from Gerald Tsai, one of the best known wizards of Wall Street. Gerry Tsai preceded many of the current crowd of takeover artists, using pure old-fashioned analytical skills based on fundamentals in acquiring companies or buying stocks. Before he left the Wall Street scene, Gerry Tsai ran American Can Co., which later became Primerica, the predecessor of global giant Citigroup. Cynthia Tsai says she learned from one of the "masters on Wall Street, about buying value in companies below their intrinsic worth." And one of the "fruits of my Wall Street experience was buying Time Warner stock when nobody wanted it, and at quite a bargain."

Anytime such a towering, high-profile icon finds itself on the ropes, it should merit investor attention and deep analyses of its long-term prospects. First of all, Time Warner owns diversified interests and assets in publishing, filmed entertainment, cable systems, television networks, and the Internet through its AOL unit. In publishing, its flagship Time Inc. has more than 130 magazines worldwide, including *Time, Fortune, People*, and *Sports Illustrated*.

A number of Time's smaller magazines were put on the block as part of the company's restructuring and cost-cutting. Time Warner Cable serves 14 million subscribers, and it provides high-speed data, digital video, and digital voice over Internet Protocol phone. In Hollywood, Time Warner also rules with its Warner Bros. and independent New Line Cinema studios. Some of its movie franchises are *Batman*, *Harry Potter*, and *Lord of the Rings*. In cable, Time Warner's crown jewels include CNN, HBO/Cinemax, Turner TNT, and TBS Broadcasting. In September 2006, Time Warner's WB broadcast network merged with CBS's UPN to form CW Network.

Time Warner's stock has had a storied past. Since 2002, when it tumbled to around $8 a share, the stock crawled ever so slowly, but it reached $18 by 2004. And then the activist investor Carl Icahn discovered the stock and started buying shares in 2005. No longer was Time Warner a wallflower. Time Warner turned out to be a home run for Cynthia Tsai and other investors who loaded up on the stock at $8 and $9. Admittedly, it took several years for it to round home plate.

But even though Time Warner stock has gained some momentum, it is still not one of the popular or, more to the point, attractive stocks in the estimation of many professional investors. Time Warner today is still within that group of potential big winners, I am convinced. Its stock remains attractive because of the company's vast opportunities to grow robustly. The stock still belongs to the "potential winners" category, still in the bench-warmer's corner waiting to play in the all-star games again.

On March 31, 2006, I wrote a story on *BusinessWeek* Online suggesting that it was "bounce time" for Time Warner, then trading at $17 a share. I suggested that the smart thing to do was to buy the long-languishing stock before the big investors caught on—or became convinced—that some significant moves were about to take place.

At that time, Icahn had come to terms for a rapprochement with Parsons, who had agreed to do a $20 billion buyback. One of Icahn's big campaigns was to push management to split up Time Warner by selling its cable operations. Parsons rejected splitting up the company, although it filed registration papers to take public part of its cable business, primarily its assets in Adelphia, which it acquired jointly with Comcast in July 2006. Time Warner ended up with 84 percent of Adelphia.

To back up my bullishness—I was very much a lonely voice then—I suggested in the column that there were plans to take Time Warner's cable operations public. Time Warner finally did take the cable unit public by selling 16 percent to the public in 2007. The year before, Time Warner sold some assets to raise cash, including its book publishing business for $532 million. As for AOL, Google paid $1 billion for a 5 percent stake in the giant Internet portal unit. I figured that either Google would raise its stake in AOL or it would try to convince Parsons and the board to take AOL public. By selling just 20 percent of AOL, it could fetch $4 billion, according to some analysts' estimates.

The stock rallied because of early signs of a turnaround at AOL. Indeed, Time Warner has shown encouraging signs of an earnings recovery. The company lost money in 2001 and 2002 and then posted a measly 68 cents a share in 2003 and an equal amount in 2004. In 2005, things got worse, with earnings dropping to 62 cents. Analysts expected earnings of $1.03 a share for 2007 and $1.16 in 2008.

Wall Street has come around to embracing the stock. On September 2007, 18 of the 24 analysts who follow the once-disdained company recommended buying the stock, while six rated it a hold. None recommended selling the stock. That was quite a turnaround for the analysts. They were convinced that Time Warner was determined to make the company an influential "first force" in all of its lines of business, primarily in the fields of cable and filmed entertainment. On the Web, Time Warner's plans are formidable: It aims to use AOL's worldwide reach, with 17.7 million subscribers in the U.S. and 5.5 million in

Europe as of September 30, 2006, to expand into other Internet services. Part of the goal is to expand AOL's search partnership with
Google. AOL hungers to come back and recapture its once powerful
place on the Web. Analysts are optimistic that AOL's new strategy to
focus aggressively on the rapid growth of online advertising—in part
by providing its subscribers free access services, such as e-mail—will
win new adherents to AOL.

Cost-cutting in its worldwide operations, buttressed by merger
deals, particularly in its cable enterprise, were part of Dick Parson's
plans for growth.

Parson knew that Carl Icahn and his ilk would never be out of the
picture, especially if management failed to dramatically lift the Time
Warner enterprise from the ground.

The activist shareholder started buying Time Warner shares in
the first quarter of 2005, when the stock was at about $18. Icahn and
his partners—Franklin Mutual Advisers Inc., Jana Partners LP, and
SAC Capital Advisors LLC—accumulated shares totaling 2.6 percent
in the second quarter of 2005. Icahn's group tried to stir up investor
enthusiasm for Time Warner by proposing drastic changes, including
splitting up the company and increasing its stock repurchase plan to
$20 billion. Parsons rejected the idea of a breakup but agreed to
boost the company's share buyback to $20 billion, and to reduce
expenses by $1 billion over two years. On February 16, 2007, Carl
Icahn cashed out part of his winnings on his Time Warner stake, making a profit of at least $250 million. He sold stock worth $880 million
in the fourth quarter of 2006, reducing his stake to 25 million shares
from about 69 million in that period.

Shares of Time Warner's cable division, called Time Warner
Cable, now the second largest cable company in the U.S., started
trading on the New York Stock Exchange on March 1, 2007, almost
two years after Time Warner agreed to buy assets from bankrupt

Adelphia Communications, Inc. About 16 percent of the cable company, representing shares owned by former creditors to Adelphia, now trade under the ticker symbol TWC. The stock's trading ended a chapter that started on April 1, 2005, when Time Warner and Comcast Corp. agreed to buy Adelphia in a joint bid. Time Warner retained the remaining 84 percent of TWC, its fastest growing unit. Time Warner Cable owns and manages cable systems linking approximately 26 million homes in 33 states. The company has 14.6 million customers for its various products, which include video, high-speed data, and residential telephone. Its customer base includes approximately 13.4 million basic video subscribers and more than 6 million customers who purchase more than one product.

Speculation about Time Warner being broken up by spinning off some of its many assets has not abated. Some argue that after taking the cable operations public, the next logical move would be to spin off other units. Parsons had publicly rejected such a move. The fact that Time Warner is performing well convinced him that keeping the company intact was the way to go.

In early November 2007, Time Warner announced that Parsons will step down as CEO on January 1, 2008, to be replaced by Time Warner President and Chief Operating Officer Jeffrey Bewkes. For investors seeking to participate in the growth of a giant media conglomerate, Time Warner is a terrific bet for the long term. That idea got a lift on November 4, 2007, when Time Warner announced a change at the top. Bewkes has yet to announce his plans as of mid-November 2007. However, there is a lot of speculation that Time Warner might finally get unstuck from its years of underperformance. So far, Parsons is to remain chairman, but rumors abound that Bewkes will end up getting that chairmanship as well. Although the stock didn't react much to the announcement, Wall Street expects some big changes at Time Warner in 2008.

Bewkes, who is the architect of Time Warner's efforts to boost its AOL unit, is expected to take measures that would unlock the intrinsic value of the company, which should push up the stock's price.

Here are some possible moves by Bewkes to achieve that goal: Take AOL public by spinning off to shareholders some 20% of the company, thus creating a separate independent value for AOL. An alternative would be to merge AOL with another major portal like Google, which already owns 5 percent of AOL, or Yahoo. Google, on the other hand, might simply decide to buy AOL. Apart from taking AOL public, selling it, or merging it with another Internet company, Bewkes might also decide to spin off Time Warner's publishing operations, again to unlock the unit's value, as an independent or publicly traded entity. The idea behind all of this restructuring is for investors to be able to determine the true value of Time Warner on a sum-of-the-parts valuation. That valuation will be much higher than the stock's current price.

If Bewkes pursues any of these moves, excitement will once again come to Time Warner and very likely enliven its stock. "The bad press masks [Time Warner's] great business," notes Value Line's Rueben Gregg Brewer, who says there are many positives hidden within the media giant. Owning the pipes into peoples' homes, as well as the content that flows over those pipes, "is a solid model," says Brewer. He says the pieces are in place for "decent share-price appreciation over the three-to-five-year pull." Time Warner's stock closed at $16 on December 28, 2007, a 52-week low, and down from its high of $22.96 on January 18, 2007. Time Warner is a company that should see sunshine starting in 2008.

Merck: A Prescription for Winning

Merck, the fourth largest U.S. drug maker, has gone through painful and difficult times in the past couple of years, causing many investors to unload their shares when they sniffed early signs of trouble. But you could have doubled your money in a year if you had the foresight, guts, and analytical wisdom to envision that Merck, even when it was in deep trouble, had the resources and determination to overcome its king-size problems—and win.

The company hasn't proclaimed victory, but the strong recovery and release of its stock from the emergency room is already a victory for a stock that had been diagnosed as practically dead. Merck's troubles started some three years ago when it was forced to withdraw its big-seller painkiller Vioxx from markets worldwide because of cardiovascular side effects that scared not only Wall Street but also Main Street. The concern over Vioxx unleashed an avalanche of lawsuits against Merck from people and families who claimed they were severely harmed, or the family members were killed, by the painkiller. According to Merck, 14,200 lawsuits were filed as of June 30, 2006, alleging personal injuries from the use of Vioxx. That number had grown to about 27,000 cases as of December 16, 2006. In September 2004, Merck pulled Vioxx, a Cox-2 inhibitor for pain and arthritis that generated 11 percent of Merck's sales, off the market after studies linked it to increased risk of heart attacks.

We will look at how Merck triumphed in spite of the lawsuits, even before its agreement with the plaintiffs' lawyers to settle the ugly and expensive chapter in Merck's history. On November 12, 2007, Merck reached a $4.85 billion settlement deal.

Merck's stock, which traded as high as $97 a share in 2000, had dropped in 2004 to around $50. Besieged by thousands of lawsuits, Merck plummeted to as low as $25 by the end of 2004. The stock traded within a narrow range, between $25 and $35, during all of

2005—evidence that in spite of all the bad news surrounding Merck, some courageous souls still bought the stock for quick, short-term gains. Some of the trading, of course, included pros who were selling the stock short. It was at that precise price point that the stock became a tremendous buying opportunity.

By the end of 2005, the stock showed glimmers of life and started to edge higher—to $31 a share, and then upward to $43 by year-end 2006.

What happened to the lawsuits at that point? The bad news for Merck was they had not gone away. The good news was that Merck had won, by then, 8 out of 12 litigated cases.

When Vioxx and the plaintiffs' lawyers agreed on a settlement, some 30 percent of the 27,000 lawsuits were pending in the federal courts, with 60 percent in New Jersey, where Merck is headquartered. Pfizer, which makes a similar pain reliever called Bextra, withdrew its drug from most markets in April 2005 because of FDA concerns about its safety.

Judging by the thousands of lawsuits that Merck had to tackle, the drugmaker's troubles looked overwhelming from every angle. Some of them involved very serious allegations, including the death of 44-year old Brian Hermans attributed to Vioxx. The first phase of the trial in the case, in a Superior Court in New Jersey, focused on whether Merck failed to warn doctors about the risks of the drug, and whether the company violated New Jersey's Consumer Fraud Act in the way it marketed Vioxx.

Hermans' family members contend that he died after taking Vioxx for 19 months to relieve pain in his knee. An autopsy showed that Hermans, a former Wisconsin state racquetball champ, suffered a heart attack, arrhythmia, and blood clot in the heart. Merck, on the other hand, contends that Hermans suffered from an enlarged heart and diseased coronary arteries, exacerbated by a family history of heart disease and early death. The company maintains that Hermans died from arrhythmia. Superior Court Judge Carol Higbee, on January 19, 2007, ordered Merck to expunge a press release it had issued that stated Hermans had methadone in his blood when he died.

For Merck, one positive sign had surfaced: Its stock had been on the rise since some analysts, who had abandoned Merck after Vioxx was pulled off the market in September 2004, came back to voice more pleasant comments about the company. The analysts recommending a "buy" or "overweight" on the stock increased from a year ago. Some of them posted bullish ratings as early as July 2005, when the stock had dropped to $26 a share.

I had been watching Merck since the start of its Vioxx woes, and my gut feeling told me that I should write a story about the pummeled stock once a glimmer of hope flashed, indicating Merck would emerge in one piece from its long nightmare. On July 25, 2005, I wrote my story. The nightmare wasn't over at the time, but all indications were that Merck would survive the attack.

"Beleaguered Merck May Be Laying Its Vioxx Woes to Rest." That was the headline in the "Inside Wall Street" column in *Business-Week's* issue of July 25, 2005. It was quite an aggressively optimistic headline at the time, when lawsuits against Merck had started to surge. But I had my sources who abided by the Buy the Losers commandment.

I noted in my story that although most Wall Street analysts remained bearish, some investors were getting more courageous and optimistic about Merck—and applying the dictum that to win, you have to buy early when nobody likes the stock. Investors started buying shares. The stock moved up on November 9, 2004 from $26 to $31 a share.

One of my sources for the story was Carl Birkenbach, president of Birkenbach Securities Management, who makes it his rule never to buy a stock on its way up—whether it is a large or small-cap stock.

He recalled the opportunity he saw in Merck, which was then an underdog and its stock a loser. Despite the "negative aura" surrounding the stock, he said, he was convinced Merck would beat analysts' reduced 2006 consensus earnings forecast of $2.41 a share. Since then, consensus estimates have risen.

Merck was trading at a "fire-sale price," said Birkenbach. It was, of course, reflecting the many lawsuits that Merck faced, but it did not, in his mind, take into account the new drugs in the company's pipeline—and the possible return of Vioxx. Among Merck's new drugs were Gardasil, a treatment for cervical cancer, and Januvia, for diabetes.

Another source I quoted in the story was Michael Krensavage of Raymond James & Associates, one of the rare Merck bulls at the time, who rated the stock a "strong buy." His target for the stock was $42. On September 2007, the stock soared to $50. Standard & Poor's analyst Herman Saftlas, who recommended the stock as a buy in September 2007, commended top management for its handing of what he considered daunting Vioxx litigation. He also praised management for coming up with new important products, such as Gardasil and Januvia, and cutting down costs.

Merck had a host of other problems apart from its legal issues. Revenues and earnings in 2006 were affected by the loss of patients who were on several important drugs. Its flagship and largest selling drug, Zocor, a cholesterol-lowering drug with annual sales of $4.3 billion, faced generic competition after its patent expired in June 2006. And the legal costs associated with the lawsuits and litigations took a heavy toll on Merck's sales and profit margins.

One impressive thing about Merck is that it has been able to sustain profitability throughout its long ordeal. Merck's total revenues in 2004 of $22.9 billion dropped to $22 billion in 2005, and in 2006, they were $22.6 billion, slightly above earlier forecasts of $21.2 billion. Net income suffered as well, but not altogether as badly as had been expected. Merck reported 2006 net income of $4.4 billion, or $2.03 a share, versus 2005's $4.6 billion, or $2.10 a share. For 2007, Goldman Sachs expected Merck to earn $6.4 billion, or $3.15 a share on sales of $24.2 billion. For 2008, Goldman estimated earnings of $7.4 billion, or $3.43 a share on sales of $24.6 billion, and for 2009, it forecasts earnings of $8.4 billion, or $3.89 a share on sales of $25.8 billion.

Fortunately for Merck, its arsenal of new drugs allowed it to keep everything close to being balanced as best as possible. Among them: Cozaar/Hyzaar, a treatment for high blood pressure, which produced sales of $3.2 billion; Fosamax, a drug for osteoporosis, which produced sales of $3.2 billion; and Singulair, Merck's treatment for asthma and seasonal allergic rhinitis, which generated $3 billion. Merck's other drugs were equally important: antihypertensive Vasotec/Vaseretic; Crixivan, a protease inhibitor for treatment of HIV; and Proscar, a treatment for enlarged prostates. Merck also makes over-the-counter medications, such as Pepcid AC, marketed through a joint venture with Johnson & Johnson. In addition, it has a joint venture with Astra AB of Sweden, through which it sells Prilosec and other Astra drugs.

Management's handling of the daunting Vioxx litigation, new products, cost cutting, and aggressive restructuring are expected by some analysts to result in estimated savings of $5 billion by 2010.

Merck has not given up its fight to bring back its version of Cox-2 inhibitors to the market. The company has announced plans to seek the approval of the Food and Drug Administration for Arcoxia, a Cox-2 painkiller that Merck already sells in Europe and other countries outside the U.S.

Even before Merck reached a settlement on the lawsuits, Merck's legal victories had worked to ease the anxiety of investors on the issue of a potential financial catastrophe. And Merck has redeemed part of its image, convincing buyers that it did not willfully disregard its obligation to the public. Analyzing the kind of damage Merck faces, some analysts estimate that the drugmaker's ultimate financial liability will likely be in the neighborhood of $5 billion to $10 billion, far less than the earlier gloomy estimates of $20 billion to $40 billion, and deemed manageable.

Merck's stock still represents decent total return potential 2009 through 2011. The bottom line: Merck has proven that companies that find themselves in the "losers" corner because of unusual circumstances can still end up winners, given a seasoned management endowed with a clear vision for growth and valuable products. The stock closed on December 28, 2007 at a 52-week high of $58.71, way up from its previous high of $38.15 on June 28, 2007. Considering that Merck traded as high as $96.70 a share in 2000, with an annual average p/e of 25, versus a p/e of 18 on January 7, 2008, it is a long-term loser and could still rebound to its old high.

Other Fallen Angels Ready to Fly

Research In Motion, Merck, and Time Warner are shining examples of "fallen angels," or big losers, that re-emerged as resilient comeback winners. Which companies are now out there "in the cold," that have stumbled and are down for the count—but that have a fighting chance to recover and turn up as victorious gladiators?

Ford Motor (F), General Motors (GM), and Motorola (MOT) stand out among the strong candidates to become champions over the next two to four years. Right now, they are not exactly winning the popularity contest on Wall Street. But, over the long haul, they have great chances of prevailing as big winners.

Ford: Not Destined for the Scrapyard

One stock that many believe is already in the emergency room and could end up as a candidate for the scrapyard is Ford Motor Co. Number one automaker General Motors Corp. is also in dire straits, but Ford is in a graver situation.

By now, everybody knows the struggles and woes of Ford, one of America's great icons. The company experienced its worst year in 2006, when it reported a loss of $12.7 billion. In the fourth quarter alone, Ford posted a $5.8 billion loss. Apart from falling sales of its top vehicles, such as pickup trucks and sport utility vehicles (SUVs), Ford had to absorb one-time charges for buyout of employees in the course of its cost-cutting plans. It is now in the midst of cutting 44,000 jobs and shutting down about 16 plants.

Ford's share of the U.S. car market shriveled from 25 percent in the 1970s to 17.5 percent in 2006. Some analysts believe things will get worse for Ford before they get better. No wonder then that of the 16 analysts who track Ford, as of September 30, 2007, five recommended selling the stock, eight rated it a "hold" or "neutral," and only three advised buying it.

Over a year ago, before he gave up the position of CEO of Ford, William Clay Ford Jr. vowed that the car maker would "reclaim its legacy" in the industry and emerge stronger than it had ever been. That hasn't happened—yet. But there are some investors who are buying shares at these low levels, convinced that Ford won't fall by the wayside or file for bankruptcy.

For such investors who believe Ford will, indeed, turn around, perhaps in two or three years, the stock's price is certainly right. From its 52-week high of $9.64 on July 2, 2007, the stock has eased to $6.70 on December 28, 2007, a 52-week low.

William Clay Ford Jr. gave up the post of CEO in the autumn of 2006 and recruited Alan R. Mulally, Boeing Co.'s chief executive, for the job. The new man at the top has been busy trying to make Ford's promise happen. Mulally has formulated an impressive "Way Forward" recovery plan, in which he demands a weekly, instead of the usual monthly or semiannual, report on progress that's being achieved with his turnaround strategy. Observers believe Mulally is getting up to speed quickly. Although lacking experience in the automotive industry, Mulally is regarded highly and is well qualified. At Boeing, the problems were as king-size as those at Ford. Mulally is credited with the giant aerospace company's turnaround.

The only analyst who was daring enough to be bullish on Ford at the time was Jonathan Steinmetz of Morgan Stanley, who upgraded his recommendation on the car company from neutral to "overweight." (As of August 2007, however, the analyst reclassified his rating as "restricted," which means he and Morgan may be involved in some deal pertaining to Ford.) It definitely was a thing of courage to turn bullish at the time that he did earlier. By late July 2007, another analyst turned bullish—Rod Lache of Deutsch Bank, who upgraded his rating to a buy.

Lache's switch to the bullish side was based on his expectation that Ford will achieve significant structural changes from its ongoing contract negotiations with the United Auto Workers. Steinmetz, in an earlier analysis on Ford, believed Ford has ample funds to engineer a turnaround. He estimated Ford would have over $40 billion of gross liquidity to start with in 2007, and he figured Ford in its turnaround efforts would burn some $13 billion of that by 2009, much less than Ford's expectation of a $17 billion burn.

There are plenty of signs that the new CEO has a greater sense of urgency. A dividend cut, new funding, and employee buyouts were among signs that management finally appreciated the gravity of the situation. Part of the recovery plan was deep cost cutting. Cost reductions were estimated to save some $12 billion, which is 8.4 percent of total revenues. The savings, however, might be offset by an estimated

$4 billion in price cuts, market-share loss, and increased interest payments related to the higher debt load from new financing.

So far, the savings efforts have worked. Ford surprised Wall Street with its 2007 second quarter results, which showed better than expected earnings of 13 cents a share, compared to a loss in the previous year of 73 cents. In addition to benefiting from its cost-cutting plan, Ford also benefited from strong pricing of its products in most of its markets. The results also showed that free cash flow was better than expected, at $1.8 billion. In the first six months of 2007, free cash flow stood at $2.9 billion.

According to Deutsche Bank's auto analyst Rod Lache, Ford's revenues should increase to $149.2 billion in 2008, from 2007's estimated $146.6 billion, and 2006's $143.2 billion. But those numbers are still way below 2000's revenues of $170 billion. Lache is optimistic, however, that Ford has significantly more cost-savings potential than what the company's official $5 billion savings target.

Selling its Jaguar and Land Rover segments should help Ford raise more money. And its Volvo operations might also be on the block, suggest some analysts. These measures could produce upward of $10 billion, estimates Value Line analyst Jason A. Smith. He figures Ford could be in the black, but not until 2009. Both Smith and Lache see the losses at Ford dwindling, from 2006's $1.50 a share deficit. Smith sees Ford's recovery as partly dependent on revitalizing its new vehicle launches. "We still believe Ford is capable of turnings things around."

The Ford story has another aspect to it: speculation of a merger with Toyota Motor Corp. of Japan. The speculation on such a linkup was fueled by a surprise visit by Mulally to Japan in mid-December 2006, when Toyota's chief executive, Fujio Cho, invited Mulally for a meeting. Industry observers suggest that part of Toyota's purpose behind the meeting was simple diplomacy, aimed at curbing any backlash at Toyota's continuing rise in the U.S. market, while U.S.

automakers are struggling to keep their heads above water. Analysts believe that Toyota might just outrun Ford as the number two car maker in the U.S. by 2008. Mulally and Toyota's Chairman Fujio Cho conferred for two hours and then agreed to meet again in the future, although no date has been set.

In a report by *The Wall Street Journal* on the meeting of the two car executives, dated January 22, 2007, its reporters noted that Toyota could benefit in a practical way if Ford agreed to use its gasoline-electric hybrid technology. Toyota's momentum in establishing its hybrid design as an industry standard has slowed because GM has signed up with Germany's Daimler AG and BMW AG in an alliance to develop a hybrid system of its own, which is supposed to be simpler than Toyota's. If it is able to win Ford to its hybrid design, it would advance Toyota's technology and win more support in the U.S. market. Ford and Toyota already signed an agreement in 2004 in which Ford got access to some of Toyota's hybrid patents in exchange for data on lean-burn engines.

Also a positive to such a merger is the possibility that with Toyota, Ford could reenergize the company's turnaround, probably in gaining more financing and in sharing technology and ways to produce more efficient and much cheaper automobiles. At any rate, Ford needs all the help to burnish its image as a carmaker that's back on track, with Toyota's help, and to be able to expand into more markets for its products.

When news about Mulally's meeting with Toyota's Cho hit the U.S. media in early January 2007, Ford's stock inched up, from $7.50 to around $8.30 a share. Further news on the subject could ignite the stock if a positive turn of events ensues over collaboration between Ford and Toyota. Since then, however, not a peep has come out from either of the two companies about the merger speculation.

Without doubt, Ford represents a perfect candidate for the Buy the Loser commandment. The "fallen angel" has a sure shot at bouncing back and winning the long race. The bullish case for Ford is that there will be more cost cutting than everyone expects. Ford's new products are also a source of new optimism. How much is Ford's stock worth? Most analysts think Ford will be stuck in the mud for a while, but some expect the stock to be at $20 by year-end 2010. The stock spiked to more than $9 right after Ford reported its surprise upbeat earnings in the second quarter.

On January 4, 2008, Ford's stock closed at $6.13, down from its low of $6.88 on December 13, 2006. Ford hit a 52-week high of $9.64 on July 2, 2007. Like any investment in fallen angels, investing in Ford requires close monitoring—a month-by-month monitoring, if possible—to keep track of how the company is adhering to its recovery plan. This is a long-term opportunity, but the rewards could be worth the wait.

GM: Not in No Man's Land Anymore

General Motors (GM) is another perfect example of the Buy the Losers maxim, because after bumping to a low of $19 a share on March 3, 2006, it roared back up to $36 on February 21, 2007. Investors who dared scoop up shares in March 2006 ended up as real winners. However, most GM fans have not yet fully recovered from the stock's fall from $95 a share in 2000 to $19 by 2006.

The fact that GM dug itself out of a deep hole is in itself a stalwart achievement. However, the company continues to face gargantuan problems, so one could still count it as fallen stock that could get the wind on its back and retain its title of the world's number one producer of cars and trucks.

GM's turnaround story is gaining traction, although the number one U.S. automaker is far from being out of the woods. One of its greatest accomplishments was its historic agreement on September

26, 2007 with the United Auto Workers union, which marked a new era for the auto industry. The pact was approved after a two-day strike by 74,000 UAW members. The unprecedented agreement shifted to an independent trust $51 billion in liabilities for UAW retirees' health care. The GM-UAW agreement sets into motion cost reductions that will enable GM to better compete with foreign automakers, mainly Toyota. The health care issue has been a big concern for the Detroit automakers.

GM deserves close monitoring by believers in the Buy the Losers commandment. The near-term situation at GM is improving, concede even the analysts who are bearish on the stock. Should GM beat all negative forecasts on auto sales, earnings, and cost-cutting, long-term investors who are in GM's stock for its long-awaited recovery will receive rich rewards.

Certainly, GM is no longer "in no man's land." But the bears believe there are other stocks with better risk-reward ratios than GM. Before the GM-UAW settlement, they worried about GM's relations with the union. Another issue is whether GM's market-share erosion will continue. The GM bulls say the union agreement removes a big dagger hanging over GM's turnaround plan. One reason that Rod Lache of Deutsche Bank turned bullish on GM was his expectation that GM would work out its $46 billion UAW retiree healthcare obligation. Now that that has happened, GM's stock, which hit a 53-week high of $38.15 on June 28, 2007, drove up from $34 before the GM-UAW pact to $36.70 on September 28, 2007.

Despite the GM-UAW pact, the bears remained wary because of the poor outlook for GM's sales in the U.S. However, GM's huge progress in the international markets is helping offset sales declines in the U.S. GM is improving sales in Europe, Latin America, and China, where it has formed partnerships to build cars. GM has increased capital spending to build power train capacity in Asia. But the company says its primary focus over the next few years will continue to be on increasing North American automotive cash flow. That has prompted some analysts to increase their earnings expectations for several years ahead.

GM has been busy shifting gears to improve sales in the U.S. Sales improved in the second quarter of 2007, but GM is still losing ground to Toyota and other Japanese competitors. In the U.S., GM has started investing in fuel-efficient alternatives to its current fleet of cars, including plans to launch a family of electric cars sometime in the next three to four years.

GM has introduced exciting new cars, in particular the 2008 Saturn Astra and 2008 Pontiac G8, which debuted at the Chicago Auto Show in January 2007. The Saturn model was a hit at the 2007 Detroit International Auto Show, where it captured the North American Car of the Year Award. GM's Chevrolet Silverado Truck won the North American Truck of the Year prize. If GM continues producing exciting cars and trucks, it might be able to recapture the title of the world's largest automaker.

Given all the challenges GM has confronted, GM's stock has weathered the rough roads and highways fairly well. Over the short term, analysts see it going to at least $45. Over the next three years, GM could easily triple if all goes well. It is a perfect case for obeying the Buy the Losers commandment. The stock hit a 52-week high of $42.64 on October 12, 2007. However, the housing slump and rocketing gasoline prices pulled down the stock by early January. GM closed at $23.65 on January 4, 2008. It was yet another chance to buy this "loser" at a much lower fire-sale price.

Motorola: Will It Recover Its Mojo?

Motorola is another fallen angel, but its problems aren't as overwhelming as Ford's or GM's. However, like the automakers, the world's number two cell-phone maker was in the high stratosphere once upon a time. Its stock was trading at $61 a share in 2000. By 2003, it started winding down, eventually collapsing to a low of $7. Like GM, Motorola gathered enough strength to pick itself up, driving up to $26 a share by October 13, 2006. But, unlike GM, which has managed to stay afloat, Motorola backtracked and dropped to $14.98 a share by January 7, 2008, down from $22 on November 20, 2006.

Motorola is one of the currently scorned stocks on Wall Street that, nonetheless, deserves attention because of its impressive history as one of America's leading technology companies. It has produced some of the best products in the phone business. Its efforts to constantly launch new products is noteworthy and has allowed it to go head-to-head with big rival Nokia (NOK), which is number one in the crowded mobile phone derby.

Management's failed attempt to resuscitate the company waved a flag to raider and activist Carl Icahn, who started building up a stake in Motorola in 2007.

In 2004, Motorola CEO Chris Galvin, the grandson of the company's founder, stepped down amid speculation that the board of directors asked him to leave, even though Galvin was credited with having developed the widely popular Razr phone. He was replaced by Ed Zander, whose claim to fame is having been president of Sun MicroSystems.

"Zander hadn't exactly done a stellar job at Sun, but no matter. He fast-talked the board into believing he could improve things at Motorola," noted Joan Lappin in her TheStreet.com RealMoney column on February 2, 2007. Lappin, who is president of the investment management outfit Gramercy Capital Management, Inc. in New York, wrote, "Three years later, that fast talk looked more like double talk." Zander, she added, rode the turnaround at Motorola that was already demonstrably under way when he joined the company. In addition to taking credit for things that were not his accomplishments, Zander did one thing terribly wrong, said Lappin. "He slashed spending on R&D, the lifeblood of a high-tech company with Motorola's reputation, but margins plunged anyway. This once proud company has one of the world's great brand names, which isn't something that's valued on the balance sheet, but should be."

Some analysts agreed with Lappin, who believes Motorola can't move forward with Zander in control. Motorola is not beyond repair, she argues, but it soon will be—if Zander isn't bounced from the CEO position. Will Zander get booted out, as a growing number of people are suggesting? So far, he seems secure, with the board squarely behind him. When he was appointed in January 2004, Zander became the first outsider to land the CEO seat in Motorola's 79-year history. With Zander still in the hot seat and Motorola's stock groping for a bottom, it seems the appropriate time for investors to buy Motorola's stock at its low price level. Icahn is apparently on the right track, partly because of the $15 billion cash and cash equivalents that the company nourishes in its treasury.

Icahn has urged the board to spend $11.2 billion to buy back its own shares, rather than the $8.5 billion the company intended to spend for repurchasing stock. Motorola has already repurchased $4.7 worth of stock since 2005.

Motorola needs to move fast and recover its lost "mojo" or magic for a turnaround in its markets. Competition is on the rise, not only from Nokia, Ericsson, and Samsung but also from new rival Apple Inc., which has come up with the revolutionary iPhone.

Some analysts believe Motorola can still recover with a strong turnaround for its handset unit and strong contributions from its other units. The stock is attractive and undervalued given its 30 percent pullback since November 2006. Some 66 percent of Motorola's sales come from its mobile cell phones. Unlike most other handsets, Motorola's phones are compatible with the three digital standards: GSM, TDMA, and CDMA. And Motorola has increased its global wireless handset 2007 market share to 23 percent from 2005's 8.7

percent. But in the fast-rising markets of China and India, Nokia is way ahead of Motorola in market share, holding 30 percent against Motorola's 23 percent. In India, the disparity is greater, with Nokia holding 60 percent while Motorola has a meager 15 percent.

In the meantime, Motorola's chief financial officer, David Devonshire, told analysts that the first two quarters of 2007 would be "rocky," but that the second half would "see improvements." And 2008 and beyond are expected to show even better results. That gives investors on the hunt for bargains a chance to snap up Motorola shares on the cheap. Motorola reported its first quarterly profits during the third quarter of 2007, which prompted Zander to give a positive earnings forecasts for the year that exceeded the consensus estimates on Wall Street.

Zander has been under pressure from Icahn to revive Motorola. Icahn vowed to call for Zander's dismissal by the end of 2007 if he failed to do so. On September 30, 2007, Icahn disclosed that he and his hedge funds held 3.3 percent of Motorola's stock, or 75.6 million shares, making him the third largest stakeholder in the mobile phone company. In January 2008, Zander was replaced as CEO by Motorola President Greg Brown.

Expect the three high-profile "losers" discussed in this chapter—Ford, General Motors, and Motorola—to be big winners in the years ahead. The time to buy these shares is now, and that is not based on the adage that "timing is everything." These three stocks are a buy on their fundamental merits and low valuations, not because their industry is on the rise and therefore should be bought.

We aren't believers in market timing and, in fact, the next chapter discusses the disadvantages of timing the market—and the reasons why you shouldn't follow that popular adage. Market timing, as the next chapter explains, can give your portfolio untimely indigestion.

COMMANDMENT 4

Forget Timing

"Trying to do market timing is likely not only to NOT add value to your investment program, but to be counterproductive."

—John Bogle, founder and former chairman of the Vanguard Group of Investment Companies

"Timing the market" is a widely accepted precept in stock investing. Its proponents believe that to win in the stock market, "timing is everything." Is it? This chapter discusses the issue of timing and proposes that, in fact, timing is far from everything. Timing has enough toxicity that could poison your portfolio.

Let us examine why proponents of timing are adamant in their assumption that timing is a relevant and pivotal tool for making money in the stock market. Many market pros—in particular, the market technicians who base their conclusions on chart patterns— swear by it. They advise waiting for the propitious time to buy into the market. In addition, the professional timers assume that there are specific periods when certain industries perform well and are ripe for the picking. The conditions "have to be right," argue the timers.

Market timing involves "buying the market" at specific times by buying the index funds, which replicate the components of the Dow or the S&P 500, or buying stocks in a specific industry when the timers think they are ripe for the picking.

As an example, market timers clock the economic cycle. Stocks are either cyclical or noncyclical. **Cyclical** refers to stocks closely dependent on the strength of the economy, such as department stores, railroads, homebuilding, and construction. These industries are on the timers' buy list when the economy is showing strength. Stocks that they assume are immune to such economic twists and turns are identified as **noncyclical** or, more specifically, **defensive** stocks. Companies involved in health care, for instance, are supposed to be in a defensive sector. Food stocks are also defensive, because food is a necessity. And the companies that cater to so-called "sin" or "vice" products, such as tobacco, alcohol, and gambling, are supposed to be immune to the economy's ups or downs. The argument is that spending for these products and services is neither constrained nor abetted by the economy's health. So, in times of an economic slow-down, the timers recommend these noncyclical stocks.

Some industries, according to market timers, do better in the fourth quarter or the first quarter of the year, such as the retail store chains and department stores, whose sales are particularly dependent on the holiday shopping seasons. So, market timers advise snapping up shares of retail stores or companies dependent on consumer spending during that time of the year.

Another indicator that market timers watch is the rise and fall of interest rates. These are determined by the Federal Reserve Board's appraisal of the state of the economy and its assessment of the pace of inflation. The Fed focuses on economic data and the stream of news involving consumer and producer prices, labor wage levels, and the employment-unemployment figures. Indeed, various industries, such as banks, mortgage lenders, financial institutions, and home builders, bounce around depending on the rise and fall of interest rates. They are a "buy," in the minds of the market timers, when interest rates are in a declining mode or when the Fed is perceived to be poised to cut interest rates.

Market-Timing Technicians

Underlying all of these market timing strategies is technical analysis, practiced by a group of professional market watchers who base their decisions mainly on chart analysis to track the behavioral patterns of the market and stock groups. They scrutinize the charts to determine whether the market is on its way up or down, and when or under what circumstances specific stock groups advance or lose ground.

What do the technicians look for when they are scrutinizing their charts? Trends, trends, trends. Technical analysts claim that their chart readings identify the major trends, be it the macro market picture or specific stock groups—and the precise time when such trends might reverse course. When the technicians identify a trend, they try to pinpoint when it started gaining momentum and when it began losing energy. When they see a group—say, the retailers—moving up as a group during specific periods, such as the end of the year or during holiday seasons, the technical strategists assume that they should be the group to buy during those particular times of the year. It is important to the technicians that investors stay with a trend and stay in lockstep with the tape, and not to fight the market's major movements. The popular advice, "Don't fight the tape; the trend is your friend," comes from the timing strategists.

Here is how the chartists or technicians follow the charts. When a trend is deemed to have formed, the technicians mark the boundaries of the stock's movement. The ceiling or upper limit of stock prices is marked the **resistance level**, and the lowest price line is marked the **support level**. When a stock's price penetrates or breaks through the upper resistance level, it is called a **breakout**, which is a bullish sign for the stock or stock groups. That is when the technicians issue a strong buy signal. Conversely, when a stock penetrates or breaks below the support level, it indicates a breakdown and signals a strong sell.

Jeremy J. Siegel, the Russell E. Palmer professor of finance at the Wharton School of the University of Pennsylvania, noted in his book, *Stocks for the Long Run*, that since the crash in 1987, the buy-and-hold strategy has beaten the timing strategy every year except 1995 and 1996, when the two strategies yielded equal returns. The year 2000, he recalls, was a particularly disastrous year for the timing strategy. "With the Dow meandering most of the year above and below the 200-day moving average, the investor pursuing the timing strategy was whipsawed in and out of the market, executing a record 16 switches into and out of stocks," he says.

Ignoring transaction costs, the timing strategist lost over 28 percent in 2000, whereas the buy-and-hold strategist lost less than five percent. But since 1990, the buy-and-hold strategy has returned 14.09 percent, whereas the timing strategy has returned only 7.39 percent, according to Siegel.

It is true that a number of technical analysts, who are the principal source of advice for timing the market, have developed enough expertise to make money. However, the entire issue of timing has come under criticism from several highly respected investment pros. They doubt strongly that market timing can deliver what it promises and might, in fact, result in producing disastrous results to stock portfolios.

John Bogle, a pioneer and respected leader in the mutual fund industry, rejects timing in unequivocal terms. He observed that in his "30 years in this business, I do not know of anybody who has done it (market timing) successfully and consistently."

Burton G. Malkiel, a Princeton University professor and market guru who authored the long-time best-selling book *A Random Walk Down Wall Street*, is also highly critical of market timing and technical analysis. Technical rules, he notes, have been tested exhaustively, using price data in major exchanges "going back as far as the beginning of the 20th century." He argues that the data reveals conclusively that past movements in stock prices cannot be used to foretell future movements. "The stock market has no memory," he argues. He goes even further, saying that the central proposition of charting "is absolutely false, and investors who follow its precepts will accomplish nothing but increasing substantially the brokerage charges they pay."

Malkiel believes that using technical analysis for market timing is "especially dangerous" because its practitioners could be out of the market when it suddenly rises without warning. It cannot compare, he suggests, to the long-term strategy of buy-and-hold. During the decade of the 1980s, the S&P 500 index provided a handsome total return of 17.6 percent. But an investor who happened to be out of the market in just the best ten days of the decade—out of a total of 2,528 trading days—was up only 12.6 percent. The data suggests in both relative and absolute terms that timing is not a healthy prescription for winning. It is essential repeating the point that Malkiel makes, that market timers risk missing the big infrequent, large sprints that are the big contributors to performance.

Timing: Underwhelming Results

Ace investor Peter Lynch, currently Vice Chairman of Fidelity Management and Research and member of the advisory board of the Fidelity funds, also has little patience for market timing. He observes that if it were true that market timing worked so well, full-time market timers would be all over the *Forbes* list of the richest people. Lynch says there has never been a pure market timer on that list. Lynch cites some statistics to prove that market timers don't do any better or worse than the overall market indexes. Timers who somehow got into the market at the top and those who got in at the bottom ended up with almost similar results. Lynch noted that $1,000 invested in the S&P 500 stock index on January 1 of every year since 1975 produced an annual return of 11 percent. If the same amount were invested at the peak of the market each year, the return was 10.1 percent. The same amount invested at the absolute low point produced a yearly 11.7 percent return.

Those statistics demonstrate the underwhelming results from using timing as a market strategy. They indicate that timing could very well be a waste of time and energy. If you want to capture super-charged returns, forget timing. Focus instead on picking stocks with standout prospects—and concentrate your market money on them. Market timing isn't a valid substitute for picking individual stocks based on fundamentals and other factors, including the maxims that this book recommends.

It might be fair to say that a rising tide lifts all the boats. If an industry is perceived to be facing favorable prospects, shares of all companies in that sector are supposed to benefit. However, you also have to expect that some boats have holes, and certainly those won't be lifted by the rising tide. The same principle applies in the stock market. Don't expect a stock with fundamental problems to go up.

One example of this was demonstrated in the growing business of retailing consumer electronics, personal computers, software, and appliances, including television sets, phones, and video/audio products. This group was supposed to be great buys, if you subscribed to the timing strategy, because the tide was lifting during the months before the Thanksgiving and Christmas seasons, between October 2006 and February 2007. But only two of the five major players chalked up gains despite the rising tide of business.

PC Connection (PCCC) was the best gainer, moving from $9.49 on October 25, 2006, to $18 on February 8, 2007. The other gainer was GameStop (GME), which advanced a bit from $25 to $26 during the same period. But Best Buy, the leader in the group, edged lower, from $56 to $51, and Circuit City dropped from $28 to $21. ValueVision also fell from $14 to $12.

Even if one assumes that the timing is right about buying retail stocks before the holiday shopping season between October and February, there is always the question of whether some of the boats in the group of stocks have holes.

Institutional Investors Love Timing

The biggest fans of market timing are the institutional investors. To them, timing is a convenient and necessary tool. Because of the large pool of money that they have to invest, they need to find a way to deploy it as quickly as possible, in a place that can absorb such an enormous sum of money. Necessarily, they have to play the diversification strategy to be able to spread out their money. And that's how diversification begets market timing.

Market timing is a compelling tool for the big institutions. They buy into groups of stocks to make their money "work" in the market, and what better way than to time the market? It is a way not only to invest large sums of capital but, possibly, to get lucky in calling the turns of the market. When the institutional investors believe the market's temperature to be just right, as per the advice of their favorite market technicians, they buy stocks "grande."

Predictably, the results of such a strategy are mediocre, because any winning stocks in an industry only offset the losers. In a timed and diversified portfolio of, say, 100 or more stocks, not many will come out winners. That's because investors who build up diversified portfolios end up buying the good stuff along with the bad. The best they can hope for is 50-50, or a flat performance.

Let us examine how investors would have fared had they timed their portfolios to beat the market. One industry that market timers particularly cotton up to is the retail store industry.

Retail Stores: Not Necessarily Bargains

The retail store industry is one example of what unedifying results timing begets. If investors put their money between October 2006 and February 2007 in the retailing group, they would have come out just even—if they were lucky. That is because some of the stocks in the group did well, while more of them did poorly. The retailing group had its winners. And, sure, the consumers propped up the economy. But you didn't have to bet on the entire group to get super returns. Picking the winners in any group is the key.

Target Corp. (TGT) is one example, because it was one of the big gainers in the retail store group. Not surprisingly, Target—which operates about 1,537 stores in the U.S., located mostly in California, Texas, and Florida—stayed ahead of the pack. Its stock climbed from $58 a share on October 18, 2006, to $62 on February 8, 2007. Target has a lot going for it, including a proficient and innovative management and stylish products at reasonable prices. Investors would have produced better returns had they just concentrated on Target, rather than buying the whole retail sector. Target outperformed Wal-Mart (WMT) in same-store sales increases, among other things. During the same period of October 2006 to February 2007, Wal-Mart's stock was flat at $48 a share. The other big winners in the group were Costco Wholesale (COST), which climbed from $52 to $56, and Big Lots, Inc. (BIG), which rose from $20 to $27. The losers in the group: Macy's (M), formerly named Federated Dept. Stores, which fell from $44 to $42, and Stein Mart, Inc. (SMRT), which dropped from $16 to $14. The others in the industry were flat, lackluster performers—BJ's Wholesale Club (BJ), Fred's, Inc. (FRED), Dollar Tree Stores (DLTR), Family Dollar Stores (FD), and 99 Cents Only Stores (NDN). In sum, the retail store group was nothing but a wash.

Banks: Banking on Some

Market timers who rushed into banking stocks in 2006 expecting the Federal Reserve Board to cut interest rates had a woeful awakening. It was a rocky period for interest rates, and banking stocks fared badly as a result, with only a few of them gaining some upside traction. The Fed did not roll back interest rates in 2006. Again, market timers in this group would have done much better had they snapped up the stalwarts in the industry instead of buying into the whole banking sector—with or without an interest rate reduction.

The winners in 2006 included Bank of America Corp. (BAC), JPMorgan Chase & Co. (JPM), and Wachovia Corp. (WB). The losers included Commerce Bancorp (CBH), Greater Bay Bancorp (GBBK), Popular Inc. (BPOP), and Zions Bancorp (ZION).

As a group, financial stocks don't offer much upside potential. The market timers wait for signs that the Fed will cut interest rates. And when they start to sense this, they jump in and buy into the banking sector. But there is little evidence that this strategy worked in the past and, in all likelihood, market timers won't find it a worthwhile strategy.

The Fed did reduce rates on September 18, 2007, which drove the market to new record highs. But by that time, the banking industry was already reeling from the explosion of the subprime mortgage lending problem, and the rate cuts didn't do much for the financial group. Because of the protracted housing slump and problems about subprime and the credit squeeze, the Fed in early December 2007 again cut the federal-funds rate by a quarter of a percentage point.

Analysts and market timers constantly stress over the question of whether the Fed will cut rates. The solution to the Fed interest rate question is to stay away from it by simply picking the financial companies that are worthy without depending on the grace of the mighty Federal Reserve.

The meltdown in the subprime mortgage market was an odious development for the banks, and investor sentiment has turned sour toward the group. The eroding subprime market spread into the broader mortgage and mortgage-based securities markets.

Certainly over the short term, the subprime troubles were a damaging setback for companies in the credit and housing sectors. But amid the gloom, long-term opportunities might be emerging. It is true that the subprime mortgage problems have resulted in some bankruptcies among the subprime mortgage lenders. However, the big banks, whose stocks have also been hammered, have deeper pockets, as well as diversified revenue bases that should minimize the impact. Remember one of the maxims in this book: For investors to make outsize profits, they should seize opportunities in the face of darkness.

Citigroup

The banking stocks have been a lackluster performer since 2002, and the credit crisis in 2007 only worsened the situation for the industry. But among the banks that offer attractive opportunities is Citigroup, one of the most disappointing underperformers in the group.

Citigroup was facing increasing shareholder clamor for reforms even in early 2007. The company's critics—and there were loads of them—argued that the big problem was how the company planned to get back to its growth path. They contended that there hadn't been much progress in advancing Citigroup's global franchise.

Vikram Pandit Takes the Helm

The ugly deterioration of the subprime mess overtook all those complaints, and took a heavy toll on Citigroup: On November 4, 2007, Citigroup CEO Charles Prince resigned, under pressure from the board after the company disclosed a writedown of as much as $11 billion on top of the $59 billion it had reported in the third quarter. Former Treasury Secretary Robert Rubin stepped in as chairman. Sir Win Bischoff, the head of Citigroup's European operations and the CEO of Schroders when Citigroup acquired it in 2000, was appointed the temporary CEO while the board looked for a permanent chief executive.

After a five-week search, Citigroup on December 11, 2007, named Vikram Pandit as its new CEO. Pandit was the head of Citigroup's investment banking operations. The company also named Sir Win Bischoff, who had been the acting CEO, as chairman, replacing former U.S. Treasury Secretary Robert E. Rubin who had stepped into that role when Prince resigned.

Before the disclosure of the surprise write-downs, the subprime mortgage crisis that grabbed the headlines in the summer of 2007 was the episode that pushed Citigroup's stock way down. From a 52-week high of $56.41 on December 27, 2006, Citigroup dropped to a 52-week low of $45 on September 10, 2007. Then Citigroup on October 6, 2007 announced that third-quarter earnings dropped 60 percent from a year earlier, mainly because of the $5.9 billion write-down in the value of corporate loans and mortgage-backed securities. The big third-quarter loss revived speculation that Prince's days as CEO were numbered. Early in 2007, investors complained that Prince wasn't aggressive enough to push Citigroup back to its leadership position. Considering that Citigroup's position had gone from bad to worse, Prince's hold on the throne considerably weakened. His subsequent ouster came as no surprise because of the rapid-fire disclosure of the deterioration in Citigroup's exposure to the mortgage problems.

The stock's dive in September had made it even more difficult for Prince to fend off his critics. The same board that had been supportive of Prince was, in fact, the same board that finally accepted his resignation. Several board members had been quite outspoken in supporting him prior to the disclosure of the huge write-downs. They included Alain Belda, chief of Alcoa and Citigroup's lead independent director; Andrew Liveris, CEO of Dow Chemical who joined the board in 2005; and Anne Mulcahy, CEO of Xerox.

These three supporters had suggested that Prince be allowed to continue executing a strategy. "I am a fellow CEO," said Liveris, and "all of us would appreciate a bit of patience." That sentiment was echoed by Alcoa's Belda and Xerox's Mulcahy. But that expression of support was voiced before the subprime mortgage mess. Since then, the board members have remained silent, and observers say that now, the board may be feeling uncomfortable and remorseful for not having foreseen Citigroup's mishandling of the mortgage loan mess and the big black hole that it would leave behind.

During the four years that Prince was CEO, Citigroup's stock underperformed based on almost all measures. Indeed, Prince's performance proved a disaster since he took over the helm from Sanford Weill. Weill's stewardship is credited with creating the global mammoth financial leader that Citigroup had become, through acquisitions and Weill's dogged pursuit of growth for the company. Prince, however, failed miserably to build on such growth. Among his worst decisions was purchasing in early September 2007—when the sub-prime mortgage scandal was just starting to unravel—the mortgage loan operations of Ameriquest, the biggest U.S. subprime mortgage company before it shut down. Citigroup also bought Argent Mortgage Co., an Ameriquest sister company that made loans through independent brokers. The purchase price for these mortgage operations hasn't been disclosed. What Citigroup bought was the part of Ameriquest that manages collections on $45 billion worth of loans, and the distribution of principal and interest payments to investors in mortgage bonds. Together, Ameriquest and Argent Mortgage was the number one subprime mortgage lender in the world. In early 2006, Ameriquest agreed to pay $325 million to settle predatory lending investigations by Attorneys General in 49 states and the District of Columbia. As part of the settlement, it adopted reforms aimed at pro viding more transparency and fairness in the granting of loans and property appraisals.

Down but Definitely Not Out

On November 19, 2007, the banking analyst at Goldman Sachs told investors to sell Citigroup's stock, speculating that Citigroup might have to report $15 billion in write-downs over the ensuing two quarters. The stock dived to a low of 31, its lowest in four years.

It isn't surprising that investors and analysts have turned negative on Citigroup's stock. But that isn't de facto a negative. Remember that if everybody is bullish on a stock, more often than not the price would already be reflecting such bullishness. The dominance of bear-ishness toward Citigroup might signal that the company is probably at its worst and things could only get better. The handful of analysts who continue to be high on Citigroup are confident that the company is resilient enough to overcome short-term problems, including the subprime mortgage mess.

One positive thing that Prince did before his departure was to strengthen upper management with the appointment of Gary Crittenden as the new chief financial officer, Robert Druskin as chief operating officer, and Sally Krawcheck as the CEO of the Global Wealth Management unit. For a while, that softened much of the criticism against Citigroup's management. But the situation has certainly changed since the big loss it reported for the third quarter.

In the midst of Citigroup's woes on November 19, 2007, when Goldman Sachs torpedoed Citgroup's stock, some bold and aggressive investment managers did go against the current negative tide and started buying shares of Citigroup and other financials, including Bank of America, JPMorgan Chase, American International Group, Merrill Lynch, and Morgan Stanley. One of the aggressive buyers was David Katz, chief investment officer of Matrix Asset Management, a New York money management company with assets of $1.6 billion. Katz and owns 1.2 million Citigroup shares.

Katz was aware of the risks involved, but the rewards to confronting them looked compelling. The case for buying was not based on market timing. On the contrary, it was a case of buying the troubled companies at bargain prices, companies that had huge financial resources to survive the crisis. These financial companies might, indeed, face more problems ahead. But these giant companies play a central role in the economy and will continue to have bright prospects. "We aren't playing with fire in buying their shares, because they are the biggest and best players in finance and investments with tremendous, diverse resources and healthy balance sheets," Katz says.

Katz put it appropriately when he said that Citigroup and the other financials were being priced by the market as if there had been a permanent impairment in their earning power. Citigroup was trading at the low end of its ten-year valuation.

S&P analyst Frank Braden says that Citigroup's large exposure to subprime-related assets of about $55 billion leaves open the possibility of further write-downs—should conditions worsen. He believes the appointment of Vikram Pandit as CEO provides Citigroup with a stable and capable leadership. Nonetheless, he acknowledges that righting the ship at Citigroup will likely take time. Its near-term growth might suffer, he says, as Citigroup focuses on boosting capital levels instead of making acquisitions. But he expects revenue will be bolstered by international growth and expansion in the global wealth management and transaction service businesses. Indeed, Citigroup's main objective in the first half of 2008 is to increase capital levels. "The new management team will be more willing to take aggressive action to improve Citigroup's capital position," says Braden. He has been a long-time bull on Citigroup, but on January 2, 2008, he cut his 12-month price target on the stock from $61 to $43, based on his reduced 2008 earnings forecast of $3.91 a share, mainly because of the uncertainty surrounding future write-downs.

An analyst who has remained a bull on Citigroup despite the subprime woes is Vivek Juneja of JPMorgan Securities. He says the stock is being valued below other large banks in the U.S. and close to overseas banks despite its "better global footprint for growth." Concerns about the fallout from the barrage of issues hitting the industry are behind the low valuation. But the analyst expects Citigroup's growth to improve in 2008, led by continued expansion of revenues, especially overseas, recent rise in investment spending, recovery in net interest income, and slower expense growth. These positives should offset higher credit losses and lower capital markets-related revenues, Juneja argues.

Meanwhile, Citigroup has been moving to further expand overseas, partly through combinations. In Britain, Citigroup agreed to buy Egg Banking, one of the UK's top online financial service providers. In Central America, Citigroup bought Grupo Cuscatlan, a leading financial service firm. A consortium led by Grupo has signed an agreement to purchase an 85.6 percent stake in China's Guangdong Development Bank. Citigroup will end up owning a 20 percent stake in the Chinese bank.

Given its beleaguered stock and its depressed valuation, Citigroup appears a real bargain for what it represents in assets, global presence, and increasing foothold in foreign markets. As to the problem of who will succeed Prince, it is a momentary problem that could produce very positive results. Some institutional money managers had bought shares partly in anticipation that Prince would be ousted and replaced by a more vibrant new CEO. They figure that his successor can only improve the worsening situation at the company.

The bottom line: With its depressed valuation and bright prospects for further worldwide growth—in spite of the industry's subprime woes—Citigroup stands out as a bargain selling at a fire-sale price. On January 8, 2008, Citigroup's stock closed at $27.55 a share, a steep drop from $55.20 on May 30, 2007.

Bank of America

Bank of America (BAC) is the other beleaguered giant in financial services that deserves investor attention. Fortunately for this major banking institution, it exited the subprime real estate lending business in 2001 and now operates a high-quality home equity and residential real estate portfolio. Bank of America continues to widen its reach through acquisitions. One acquisition was U.S. Trust Corp., a noted private wealth manager, which BAC bought in July 2007 from Charles Schwab for $3.3 billion. The purchase makes BAC the largest manager of private wealth, a highly profitable business. Two other acquisitions were that of MBNA Corp. in 2006 and FleetBoston in 2004. MBNA made Bank of America the largest credit card issuer in the U.S., with $140 billion in managed balances on more than 40 million active accounts.

Bank of America operates in 30 states and 44 foreign countries. It has been increasing its consumer banking in the U.S., with 5,700 retail banking centers and about 17,000 ATM cash machines. The company has set long-term targets for its three main businesses. Bank of America aims to increase yearly profits from its consumer–small business banking by six to nine percent, its corporate-investment banking by seven to ten percent, and its investment management by seven to nine percent.

Like Citigroup, Bank of America's stock was also beaten down because of the overall market decline and loss of confidence in banking stocks, exacerbated in 2007 by the credit crisis. Its stock dropped to a 52-week low of $42.82 at the height of the credit turmoil on November 19, 2007, when Citigroup was hammered by Goldman Sachs' sell recommendation. It traded as high as $55.08 on November 20, 2006. On January 8, Bank of America's stock closed at $38.41 a share, way down from $55.20 on May 30, 2007.

By keeping Citigroup and Bank of America as long-term holdings, investors will end up with significant gains in the years ahead. BAC bulls have a price target of about $63, based on the historical p/e average, vast exposure in growing global markets, and balanced banking business strategy. Certainly these two battered stocks also qualify as terrific buys under the Buy the Losers commandment discussed in Chapter 3.

The Peter Lynch Principle

Looking at how the stocks in various industries have performed, the portfolio returns of market timers haven't produced spectacular numbers. To repeat what we have said in previous chapters, there is nothing better than to cherry-pick individual stocks on their own merits—and concentrate on them, instead of "timing" the market or diversifying one's stock portfolio. The evidence is overwhelming that some of the stocks discussed in this chapter stood out as ideal examples.

Peter Lynch argues that the more industries you look at, the more opportunity you have of finding a stock that's mispriced or undervalued. If you look at ten companies, you will find one that's interesting. And if you look at twenty, you will find two, says Lynch. And even if you look at just ten companies that are doing poorly, you will find one where something concrete has happened that the stock hasn't caught up with it.

"The person who turns over the most rocks wins the game," says Lynch. "It's all about keeping an open mind and doing a lot of work." In many ways, that is how many of the successful big stakeholders operate, and it's how the insiders think.

One strategy to seriously ponder is to think like an insider. The next chapter leads you into the mysterious world of the insiders and explains how outsiders, too, can amass wealth by doing what the insiders do. Individual investors can make much headway in stock investing by following the footsteps of the successful insiders. The next chapter, "Follow the Insider," explains how to do it.

COMMANDMENT 5

Follow the Insider

"The insider has only one reason to buy: to make money."

—Peter Lynch

The insider is king. In stock investing, corporate insiders and investors with huge equity stakes have a tremendous advantage over the outsiders, especially the individual investors. This chapter's maxim, Follow the Insider, shows how outsiders can cut into that advantage by doing what the insiders do.

The professional investors—including investment advisors and private equity group, hedge fund, and mutual fund managers—pay special attention to what insiders are buying. Peter Lynch, one of the top investors of all time, formerly of Fidelity Management, acknowledges that watching the insiders helps him pick stocks that often hit home runs. (More on Peter Lynch later.)

The insider is king because, more than anyone else, he or she has the most cogent information about what a company is doing. When these insiders are buying shares, investors should be buying. And when insiders are selling, investors should beware. If you know what the insider is doing, you are more than one step ahead of the investing herd.

The Insiders' World

Let us take a good look at the exclusive world of insiders. Who are they? And why would they be important to you? The real insiders are the top brass at companies, from the chairman and chief executive down to the other officers and members of the board. Corporate lawyers, accountants, consultants and the like are also, in a sense, corporate insiders, because they are privy to what's going on inside the company. And then there is the other type of insider: investors who amass a large stake in a company. They usually own at least five percent of the company's shares outstanding. Both types of insiders are required by law to regularly inform the SEC about their holdings. These insiders' buying is usually above board, but not always, as we shall soon see. Legitimate insider trading involves buying or selling shares that insiders receive from option allocations. Sometimes, these insiders go to the open market to buy beyond their allocated options. They trade these shares under prescribed rules.

The other type of insider trading—the unlawful kind—is the one that grabs headlines when the perpetrators are caught by the SEC. Those trades are based on inside information not publicly available.

In a book I wrote in 1995, *Secrets of the Street: The Dark Side of Making Money*, I detailed case upon case of insider trading in which many of the participants made troves of money illegally. A bunch of them got into trouble with the law and ended up either paying heavy fines or going to jail, or both. But many cases of insider trading go undetected. For example, time and again heavy trading occurs in stock options—a contract that gives its holder the right to buy (call options) or sell (put options) shares of a particular stock at a specified price and time—for no apparent reason. But sure enough, over the next few days, a merger or some kind of a deal is announced.

You don't have to be an Einstein to deduce that some of those traders had some kind of inside information. Sometimes the SEC nails them, but many times the agency is unable to prove illegal insider trading. Now and then, big cases of insider trading hit the press. Despite people getting caught, however, the illegal insider trading game hasn't slowed.

The "Inside Wall Street" column at *BusinessWeek* has had several encounters since the late 1980s with what one might call the "son" of insider trading. Time and again, the perpetrators were caught. Even so, such capers that stem from the column recur almost every two or three years. Their plot was simple and went like this.

Several traders and brokers bribed people at one of the printing plants that *BusinessWeek* uses around the country to provide them with advance copies. In a couple of other cases, they bribed employees at magazine distributors to get the names of stocks featured in the column early Thursday morning, when the magazine is just coming off the press. Usually the stocks mentioned in the column rise on Friday. They buy the stocks on Thursday and sell them the next day, on Friday, when the magazine hits the newsstands. (The online version of the magazine is posted after 5 p.m. on Thursdays.)

Here is part of what the Associated Press reported on April 11, 2006, about the most recent plot to steal *BusinessWeek's* "Inside Wall Street" column:

> New York—Stanislav Shpigelman, an investment banking analyst at Merrill Lynch & Co.'s mergers-and-acquisitions division; Eugene Plotkin, an associate in the fixed income division at Goldman Sachs, Inc.; and Juan Renteria, an employee at a Wisconsin printing plant where *BusinessWeek* magazine is published, have been arrested in the scheme.

Prosecutors allege that Shpigelman, Plotkin, and Renteria engaged in two separate insider-trading schemes—one that involved six pending mergers being handled by Merrill, and one that revolved around trading 20 stocks based on the pre-publication copies of *BusinessWeek*'s "Inside Wall Street" column. The government alleged that Plotkin and [David] Pajcin engaged in a scheme in 2004 and in 2005 to make trades in companies mentioned in *BusinessWeek*'s "Inside Wall Street" column before the magazine was publicly available. As part of the scheme, they bribed Renteria and Nickolaus Shuster, another employee at the Wisconsin printing plant, to give them the names of stocks mentioned in the column, prosecutors said.

Shuster was charged in March with one count of conspiracy to commit securities fraud in the matter. As a result of the scheme, Plotkin and Pajcin and others made at least $340,000 in illicit profits, the government said. "Positive news about a company in the column can push that company's stock higher in trading on Fridays," the prosecutors said. Obviously, Pacjin and his cohorts were not corporate insiders. They were outsiders who wanted to get their hands on proprietary information illegally. On January 4, 2008, Plotkin was sentenced to nearly five years in prison. Shpigelman in January 2007 received a sentence of 37 months in prison. Pajcin has pleaded guilty to criminal charges.

A Case of Insider Trading

Here is one case where a real corporate insider traded shares based on inside information. It resulted in the insider's conviction on April 19, 2007. The insider was Joseph P. Nacchio, former chief executive of Qwest Communications International, who was found guilty of 19 counts of insider trading. The prosecution argued that Nacchio was well aware that the company's financial prospects were on the decline and accused him of selling $100 million in stock before its share price fell sharply. "He sold $100 million worth of Qwest stock when he knew about problems at Qwest—problems that people outside Qwest did not know." The prosecutor added that "the case is based on a simple principle: fairness. Corporate insiders are in a position to take advantage of information that people outside don't know."

Nacchio's lawyer, who planned to appeal, argued that Nacchio did not sell stock based on insider information. He based his projections in part on analyses by the investment banking houses Donaldson Lufkin & Jenrette and Lehman Brothers, the lawyer said. In the trial that lasted three and a half weeks, the jury acquitted Nacchio of 23 other insider-trading charges. Those cases involved his sale of stocks as part of a predetermined stock selling plan. The cases for which Nacchio was found guilty involved selling after he had meetings with subordinates who warned him about Qwest's financial woes.

The entire case centered on the issue of whether Nacchio "knowingly and willfully" sold stock while he was aware of some negative nonpublic information. Nacchio insists he felt positive about the company's prospects when he sold stock, based on contracts from several secret government agencies that Qwest was on the verge of winning. The prosecution accused Nacchio of trying to drive up Qwest's stock by resorting to questionable accounting practices, such as posting one-time revenue from swaps of fiber-optic capacity with other companies as long-term revenue.

The corporate insiders I am referring to in this book are no Joseph P. Nacchios. And their trading is perfectly legal. One investment pro who believed it was well worth watching and following the insiders is Peter Lynch, one of America's most successful investors. He was one of the important contributors to the golden image that giant mutual fund Fidelity glories in. The largest revenue producer at

Fidelity after he took the helm of its Magellan Funds in 1977, Lynch holds an unbeatable record. Magellan had assets of $22 million when he took it over. By 1990, it had grown to $12 billion. As Lynch's reputation as an ace investor spread, so did Fidelity's public image. Thirteen years after he took over Magellan, Lynch quit as its manager, to devote more time to his family. Fidelity's "whiz kid" now manages money on his own, but he remains an active consultant to Fidelity.

One of Lynch's great skills was his ability to find undiscovered, undervalued stocks. One of the many ways he uncovered value was by prowling inside the "insiders' den," digging into documents and filings to find out what corporate insiders were up to, from which he determined who among them were buying their own companies' shares. When CEOs or other senior officers buy shares of their own companies in the open market, Lynch assumed that these insiders saw their potential value. Insiders have plenty of reasons to sell—to gather funds to buy a house or pay for a child's college education. But the insider buys stock, observed Lynch, for only one reason: to make money.

Lynch saw the potential of making big money when insiders would buy a lot of their own company's stock. The simple explanation is that he assumed the insiders pretty well knew how their companies were doing, and their purchases reflected their confidence in their companies. The insider buying that caught a lot of Lynch's attention was that done in the open market, not the exercise of stock options.

Many of the large Wall Street investment firms, including Fidelity, assign groups of people solely to monitor corporate insider buying. So you should also keep your eye on companies where insiders continue to add to their holdings. It suggests that the insiders are convinced the shares are undervalued. An investor can peruse various SEC filings, either over the Internet or from such publications as Barron's, other news outlets like Dow Jones Newswires, or newsletters such as the *Vickers Weekly Insider Report*, whose postings are also available online. *Vickers* gathers filings and sells them to subscribers. (More later on how investors use *Vickers* to discover stocks that produce bountiful results.) Another online outfit, the InsiderScore.com, is an insider trading and institutional data monitoring service. It monitors insider trading activity, and its proprietary algorithm scores and filters transactions in real time and highlights the most meaningful transactions. Another Web site that tracks insiders' portfolios is Stockpickr.com, where investors can see the portfolios and latest publicly available moves of hundreds of successful pros, including Warren Buffett and George Soros. Another site with similar services is GuruFocus.com, which process the batch of information to make it easier for individual investors to decipher. Remember: Insiders file 13D forms when they accumulate five percent or more stakes in a company and update them regularly, thus providing a record of their activities.

Keep an Eye on Insiders' Pals

The professional wealth managers have one particularly savvy way of playing the insider's game. And it addresses exactly what the title of this chapter suggests: Follow the Insider. Portfolio managers who have been around and have chalked up high performance scores usually develop friendly relations with the top officers of companies they invest in. Often they become golfing partners or drinking buddies, if not actually close friends.

The bigger their investment in a company, the larger the influence these money managers have on corporate chieftains and company officers. These fund managers develop an edge in the market because of such prized connections. Of course, corporate executives don't whisper secret information to them. Suffice it to say that in these friendships, some kind of interchange of ideas and opinions creates an atmosphere of trust and a "comfort zone" on both sides. The line between private information and opinion gets blurred, and often a savvy and sophisticated investment pro can discern what could be useful. The exchange of ideas also convinces the corporate executive that he has properly helped guide his big investor/friend into justifying owning or even buying more shares. Corporate execs have their interests to serve and protect, and so do the influential investment managers. Their interfacing produces good business networking. They need one another to progress and prosper.

Many of my sources for my "Inside Wall Street" column are wealth managers and CEOs. Often they inform me what certain investment managers are buying or investing in. I am not the only one who benefits from such rapport with money managers and CEOs. Other financial writers do the same thing to obtain meaningful information. The bottom line in such a give-and-take scenario is that both sides feel justifiably informed about each other's backyard. Almost no one nowadays—conscious of the required full-disclosure rules and the much ballyhooed Sarbane-Oxley law—would be caught divulging nonpublic material information to another, not even to spouses. But then again, in their friendly social banter, smart and seasoned investment pros can put pieces together and get a good idea of what's going on.

Not many individual investors can get to know insiders that closely, and even if they do, it is almost sure they won't get information from them. But what you could do is to find out what the investment pros (who are friendly with corporate insiders) are buying or accumulating. This is where Web sites tracking the portfolios of insiders, such as Stockpickr.com, comes in handy.

You need to keep up with the business news, too. Newspapers and news magazines, as well as newswire services such as Reuters, Bloomberg, Dow Jones, and the Associated Press, usually report the activities of corporate insiders and such people. They carry a lot of stories about corporate executives and money managers and who they interface with. Magazines, such as *Portfolio*, *Vanity Fair*, or even *Esquire* and *GQ*, feature stories on celebrities and their affluent friends, including top wealth managers, CEOs, and other wealthy people. On the Internet, Yahoo.com and Google are among the online services that provide all kinds of financial news and gossip on investment managers. And if you Google any of them, you will get information on corporate insiders and, possibly, who they pal around with. Your broker or financial advisor can also provide some ideas on which portfolio managers are "close" to corporate executives. The experienced brokers love to tell stories about their big clients, including what they are buying and the important people they hang around with.

Usually the portfolio holdings of the more prominent money managers are easy to track because of their document filings with the SEC. Buffett and Soros easily come to mind. Hedge fund guru Soros owns several investment funds that invest in various areas, including little known biotechs. Not all of the stocks in Soros' portfolios come up as spectacular winners, but his sharp portfolio managers have achieved enviable records, and it is worth the time to look at what stocks they own. The funds are mostly under the umbrella of Soros Fund Management. Here again, the SEC filings are the best sources of information. Investors can look up their filings on the Internet or the services I have mentioned earlier that specialize in providing such information. Edgar Online Research Services is one reliable source, either online or through offline subscriptions.

The Warren Buffett Watchers

The portfolio of Warren Buffett's Berkshire Hathaway, Inc. is, of course, a must-know because it has demonstrated solid performance time and again. However, be prepared to stay with Buffett's stocks for the long haul, because he is a devoted long-term investor. He is a marathon runner that way, expecting to win over the long stretch— over five years at the very least.

Buffett's move that surprised a lot of people was his acquisition of a 10.9 percent stake in Burlington Northern Santa Fe Corp. (BNI) in 2007, making Berkshire Hathaway the biggest shareholder in the second largest U.S. railroad company. The purchase was made public on April 6, 2007, when the stock was trading at $82 a share. Burlington Northern delivers about 45 percent of rail traffic in the West and about 23 percent of all U.S. rail traffic across 28 western and midwestern states and two Canadian provinces. Buffett's investment into Burlington Northern, of course, pushed the stock up to a new high of $94.76 by May 17, 2007. Predictably, some profit taking took place a week after Buffett's purchase. And as fear of a recession took hold toward the end of the year, the stock dropped some more, closing at $83.30 on December 28, 2007.

Buffett has a history of buying big chunks of shares in companies that he thinks are sound investments that promise big returns. Individual investors who failed to follow Buffett's move into the railroads can still get in. Remember: Buffett holds on for the long term, so he expects Burlington to go much higher over the long haul. You can bet that all the Buffett loyalists have already jumped on board. In his filing with the SEC about his purchase of shares in Burlington Northern, Buffett stated that he was also buying into two other railroads, although he didn't identify them. That raised much speculation as to which companies Buffett was referring to.

The other railroads rumored to be in Buffett's buying list were Union Pacific (UNP), the largest of the U.S. railroads, and Norfolk Southern (NSC), the fourth largest. Union Pacific's trains haul a variety of goods, including agricultural, automotive, and chemical products across the U.S. and parts of Mexico. Its stock hit a record high of

$112 on April 12, 2007—four days before the Buffett purchase was disclosed. Did some people get wind of what Buffett was doing? Probably so, because the stock was trading at around $97 in early March 2007 and then started driving up, closing at $110.46 on April 17, 2007. On October 23, 2007, Union Pacific hit a new high of $129.96. At year-end of 2007, the stock closed at $127.73.

The jump in the price of railroad shares validates the Follow the Insider maxim. Norfolk Southern's stock followed the same upward pattern. It leaped from $46 in early March and went straight up to $57, a new high, by April 10, 2007—six days before the Buffett disclosure. By June 1, 2007, the stock was at new high of $58.64. Norfolk's railroad system travels through the U.S. southeastern and midwestern states and the Canadian province of Ontario. The company also owns coal, natural gas, and timber resources in the U.S. On December 28, 2007, the stock closed at $51 a share.

The strange thing about all this is that Wall Street appeared asleep at the wheel on the railroad stocks. For instance, S&P analyst Kevin Kirkeby, on April 10, 2007, issued a report recommending a sell on Burlington, on the grounds that he expected revenue growth to slow down after three years of growth exceeding 15 percent. He thought the best the stock could be worth based on his earnings model was $80 a share. His report on the stock came two days before the Buffett purchase was disclosed.

In the case of Union Pacific, analysts weren't too enthusiastic, either. Of the 17 Street analysts who track Union Pacific, 12 had hold or neutral recommendations, and 5 had issued buys. On Norfolk, there were seven holds, seven buys, and one sell. This again demonstrates that following the insiders or big investors, such as Buffett, pays huge rewards.

Great attention has been focused on the railroads, and they appear to be good buys, in part because of Wall Street analysts' ho-hum sentiment toward them—and, of course, Buffett's positive vibes about the group. Don't be surprised if, one day, Berkshire ends up owning Burlington or another railroad company, outright. Boys played with trains when they were young. Buffett continues to play with trains in a much larger and money-making fashion. Individual investors would do well to ride on his coattails.

Warren Buffett Wannabes

A number of investment managers who aren't yet of the star celebrity caliber have become successful largely because they "custom-tailor" their style of investing after those of the big insiders. These money managers don't mind publicly proclaiming that they are, indeed, Buffett loyalists. Among them: Edwin Walczak, who heads Bank Vontobel's USA investment unit, and Douglas Davenport, president of Atlanta Investment Counsel. They have patterned their portfolios after that of Buffett, popularly referred to as the Wizard of Omaha. In fact, their holdings can be described as virtually clones of Berkshire Hathaway's portfolios.

Stephen Leeb is another wealth manager who swears by Buffett's approach and style. "I am a tremendous fan and follower of Warren Buffett, although I am basically a rabid growth investor (Buffett is a deep value investor)," says Leeb, who is president of Leeb Capital Management and The Leeb Group in New York. Their portfolios are stuffed with Buffett-type U.S. and international stocks. Leeb is one source of information about what is in Buffett's portfolios. Leeb is also editor and publisher of an investment newsletter, "The Complete Investor," and has written six books, including *Technology Defined*, published in 2000, in which he warned about a "technology crash." Technology stocks did collapse when the Internet bubble burst in late 2000, spilling over into 2001 and 2002. Leeb wrote another book in 2004, *The Oil Factor*, in which he forecast the sharp rise of crude oil prices. Crude oil prices did start to move up in 2005 and blasted off to as high as $78 a barrel in 2006, from $20 to $30. Leeb continues to warn about oil prices going even higher, to as much as $200 a barrel in three years. He isn't too far off that forecast. On November 7, 2007, oil prices rocketed to $98.62 a barrel, a record high on the New York Mercantile Exchange. Oil closed the year a hair below $100.

As an alternative to actually looking up Buffett's portfolio picks, you could check out the portfolios of these Buffett loyalists. (Leeb portfolio's performance, for one, has been on the top one percent percentile since March 31, 1999, as tracked by PSN among 250 portfolio managers in the large-cap growth sector.)

It is almost predictable that when one big investor, like Buffett, buys into a company, other big investors tend to follow. One explanation: When a noted investor acquires a large stake, he is presumed to have done extensive research and analysis. All the fundamental and technical research has been done by the early-bird investor. Thus, a second investor doesn't have to duplicate that initial research. There is sufficient reason to trust the judgment of the first large investor, at least initially. This is the reason why there are usually at least two investors who vie for the same prize in a takeover battle, as was the case in the bidding for Tribune Co. in early 2007, when Sam Zell and Ronald Burkle were bidding to acquire the media company, owner of several major newspapers, including *The Los Angeles Times*, *Chicago Tribune*, and *New York Newsday*. Sam Zell, the real estate mogul, eventually won the battle for Tribune, with an $8 billion offer.

For example, when activist investor and one-time corporate raider Carl Icahn starts accumulating shares in a company, it creates a lot of buzz and excitement on Wall Street. Other investors who stimulate widespread interest when it becomes known that they are buying stocks include Leon Black, Steven Cohen, Mario Gabelli, Peter Lynch, Henry Kravis, George Soros, T. Boone Pickens, Michael Price, Steven Schwarzman, Edward Lampert, and Nelson Peltz.

From what I have observed over the years, companies where investors own stakes of five percent or more usually end up as takeover targets. If they don't, you can bet your bottom dollar that their stocks will rocket after a year or two. I have written about many such companies in my *BusinessWeek* column—about intriguing situations involving big investors whose goal is to put companies "in play." They call attention to companies that they deem to be undervalued, and therefore potential acquisition candidates. Activist investors often become directly involved in pressuring management and the board to take immediate action to enhance shareholder value, or sometimes they seek participation (by seeking a seat or two in the board) in mapping out the company's future. In either case, it is a boon to all shareholders, because the price of the company's stock catches fire when word of a battle starts spreading.

On other occasions, big investors buy blocks of a company's shares to challenge management. These insiders declare in 13D filings that they intend to "maximize shareholder value," or to speak to management about exploring strategic alternatives. All these are indications that they want the company to put itself on the block. And when a big investor approaches the company with a plan to buy large amount of shares in a private deal, it is another signal he wants to put the company "in play." There are several reasons why the management of a company might agree to such a private stock transaction. For one, the company might need cash badly. In most private deals, the new investor agrees to pay a higher price for the stock than what it is selling for. Another reason might be that senior management believes the new shareholder would be a strategic and financial ally.

When a CEO sniffs that the investor will go out of his way to buy shares of the company, the CEO might as well cooperate with the investor and try to avert a hostile showdown. Sometimes that tactic works, but other times it just aggravates the situation. The outsider gets his foot in the door and finds out more of what's going on—which supplies him with more ammunition to advance a secret plan. After the investor is in, he usually starts buying more shares in the open market—another warning sign that there will be more to this new investor's chess move. These types of investors are usually wily and cunning.

Once in, some of these insiders decide to convince management to buy their holdings. These days, that is a difficult issue because of corporate governance rules. Nonetheless, such an expression by the big investor to unload his stake can only lead to more trouble for management. The investor's real goal is to alert management to a possibility that he could sell his stake to a third party who may be interested in buying the company.

Pressure from Big Stakeholders

Some large stakeholders tend to pressure management by saying that they are "reviewing" strategic alternatives for their shareholdings. That is another warning that this investor may be talking with another group that might have designs to buy the company. I have seen this happen repeatedly. Almost inevitably, such machinations result in more headaches for management. For the individual investor, it is an opportunity to buy the shares ahead of the actual public imbroglio between the beneficial owner and the company's management—and ahead of any deal that may be forthcoming. How does the individual investor find out about these intrigues? Usually they are reported by newspapers and magazines, by television and radio commentators, or by market newsletters.

One recent example is what happened at MedImmune (MEDI), the seventh largest U.S. biotech company. In my "Inside Wall Street" column of January 15, 2007, I wrote about MedImmune. I disclosed that a big stakeholder, Matrix Asset Advisors, led by its president, David Katz, had urged management in a letter to the company to put itself up for sale. Katz's argument was that the company's performance thus far had been lackluster. Matrix owned 1.8 million shares. It urged the board to look for a strategic buyer, noting that MedImmune owned world-class products and intellectual property whose value could best be marketed by the major pharmaceuticals, like Pfizer, Merck, GlaxoSmithKline, or Johnson & Johnson. MedImmune's major products include FluMist, a nasal spray vaccine, and Synagis, an injectable antibody to treat respiratory infections in infants.

The stock was then trading at $33 a share, and Katz was convinced it was worth at least $45. A few weeks after my story came out, billionaire activist investor Carl Icahn emerged on the scene. He acquired shares and filed with the SEC that he had accumulated a 1.1 percent stake in the company. That got the price going up, to $40. Icahn demanded a seat on the board, warning management that he wanted to put the company up for sale.

On April 16, 2007, Icahn abandoned his plan for a board seat after management assured him that it would seek "strategic alternatives" to enhance its stock. The stock as of that date had climbed to a new high, at $45 a share. In June, AstraZeneca acquired the company for $15.6 billion, pushing the stock up to $57.97 a share. Many other stories like MedImmune's suggest the validity of following the insiders. There was enough time for individual investors to make good money by buying shares after the story appeared in my column.

There are examples galore of companies that ended up in takeover deals after big stakeholders started to add more shares to their holdings. Let us look at what happened to some that resulted in takeovers. Some that didn't end up in buyouts nonetheless saw their stocks rocket after corporate insiders or big stakeholders bought sizable chunks of stocks.

Wild Oats Markets, Inc. (OATS)

In February 2006, Yucaipa American, an investor group in California that already owned a stake of three million shares of Wild Oats, went into the open market to buy an additional 789,000 shares at prices averaging $12.50 a share. Yucaipa is headed by supermarket mogul Ronald Burkle, who has a history of becoming involved in takeovers in that industry. Burkle has become a celebrity investor not only because he is a billionaire but also because he is a close friend of and big political contributor to both former President Bill Clinton and Senator Hillary Clinton.

A year later, in February of 2007, Wild Oats got a cash offer for $18 a share, or $585 million, from its bigger rival, Whole Foods Markets, Inc. (WFMI), a natural-foods grocer. Whole Foods and Wild Oats were separately battling with strong competitors among the major mass-market supermarkets that had started to get into the rapidly growing natural-organic foods market. The Wild Oats–Whole Foods deal was scheduled to close in the spring of 2007, but the Federal Trade Commission stepped in and opposed the deal. It filed a lawsuit to block the deal on the grounds that the combination would hurt consumers. The FTC contended that competition in the industry would be hampered if the two companies were combined. But some analysts, including Simeon Gutman of Goldman Sachs, disagreed. They pointed out that food retail spending is increasingly spread among different formats. Gutman said, given Whole Foods' steadfast commitment to quality, that the combination would be highly beneficial for the consumer. On August 16, 2007, a federal appeals court in Washington rejected the FTC's position, saying that the agency failed to show that the combination would adversely affect consumers. In October 2007, the FTC appealed the court's ruling on Whole Food's $565 million acquisition of Wild Oats. It last traded on August 31, 2007, closing at $18.52, not far from its high of $18.63 on August 29, 2007.

PriceSmart, Inc. (PSMT)

A little-known owner and operator of 23 U.S.-style warehouse merchandising clubs in 11 countries in Central America and the Caribbean, PriceSmart wasn't making much progress, and its stock languished in the $7 to $8 a share range. But things changed by early 2005 when the founding Price family, in a flurry of transactions, acquired hundreds of thousands of additional shares, accumulating a stake of more than 25 percent. Over the following two years, Price Smart's sales and earnings started climbing and the stock, as a result, topped $20 a share. It more than doubled in price since the Price family started buying in 2005. It isn't known whether there was a catalyst, like an activist investor lurking in the background who motivated the Price family to become more aggressive in buying more shares and taking steps to propel the company's sales to higher levels. But apparently Price knew where his company was headed—up. Sales have continued to grow and, as of late June 2007, the stock was in the mid $20s. The stock hit a new high of $33.30 on December 26, 2007.

Oakley, Inc. (OO)

An innovative designer and maker of upscale, high-performance eyewear, footwear, watches, and athletic equipment, Oakley was another company whose founder pushed up the company's fortunes by buying more shares, in addition to his already controlling stake. It was in late 2005 that James Jannard, Oakley's founder and chairman, bought an additional 1.3 million shares in the open market. Jannard's purchases between October 2005 and February 2006 ranged between $13.75 and $15.30 a share. At the time, Oakley's stock was under pressure due to the company's stagnant earnings. In less than a year, however, Oakley's revenues started beating expectations. In

2006, Oakley's sales for the year jumped 18 percent, to a record $762 million. But because of higher operating costs, earnings of $45 million, or 65 cents a share, came below 2005's $59 million, or 87 cents a share. Even so, the stock continued to climb, from $14 a share in mid-July of 2006 to $23 a share on February of 2007. Evidently, Jannard knew a lot more about the company's progress when he started buying additional shares. On July 6, 2007, Luxottica Group of Milan, the world's largest maker of eyewear, such as Channel and Prada eyeglasses, announced it was buying Oakley for $2.1 billion in cash, or $29.30 a share.

CECO Environmental Corp. (CECE)

North America's largest independent provider of air pollution control and ventilation equipment, CECO has one beneficial owner, the Harvey Sandler Trust, which owned more than one million shares. The Trust in 2005 started buying large blocks of shares in the open market, at around $2.39 a share. It continued buying through 2006, driving the stock up to $5. But the Sandler Trust wasn't through buying shares; it continued buying through 2007. So the stock kept going up and ultimately climbed to a new high of $17.72 a share on March 22, 2007. It was a big win for the Sandler Trust, and investors who followed the Trust's consistent and steady buying in 2005, when the stock was selling at just $2 to $3 a share, would have garnered huge returns. Persistent insider buying resulted in the stock's price shooting up, although there was no takeover involved. Investors interested in pollution-control companies might want to check out CECO. Its stock has come down to $11.40 a share on January 8, 2008, although 2007 third-quarter sales jumped 73%, to $65.3 million, and operating income soared 147%, to $4 million. Theodor J. Kundtz, Director of Research at investment firm Needham & Co., issued a buy recommendation on the stock on November 12, 2007.

Kos Pharmaceuticals (KOSP)

The company had been down in the dumps at $5 a share seemingly forever. But Peggy Farley, president and CEO of Ascent Capital Management, Inc., bought shares anyway in 2000. Although the company had made progress with its lead drug called Niacin, Kos was ignored for years by Wall Street and the investment community. Farley saw Kos as an incredible bargain: It had proven products, both from an efficacy and marketing standpoint; it had seasoned management with the ability to drive sales higher over time by adding new products; and it had shown capability to expand its markets. Then the stock sparkled. It climbed to an all-time high of $78 a share—yes, $78. Predictably, a lot of second-thinking and skepticism followed and, combined with predictable profit taking, the stock fell to $50. But Farley stayed with the stock, convinced that Kos couldn't have vaulted to great heights—from $5 to $78—without good reason. Sure enough, Abbott Laboratories emerged from the wings and expressed an interest to buy Kos. It eventually did, at $78 a share.

Ferreting Out Takeover Targets

Charles LaLoggia, former editor of the newsletter *SuperStock Investor*, specialized in ferreting out takeover candidates before the institutions discovered them. The *SuperStock* newsletter, published in Boca Raton, Florida, focuses on little-known companies trading well below their intrinsic value. That is enough reason to believe that they could turn out as targets, particularly when they continue to languish in spite of the good businesses they are in. What usually happens is that some of these little-known companies do attract big investors, whose buying power enables them to accumulate shares of five percent or more. Remember, when beneficial insiders accumulate more than five percent of a company's stock and file a Form 13D with the SEC, it's a signal they intend to rattle the cage to get the company's stock up.

One of the better sources of information about investors buying big blocks of stock is the *Vickers Weekly Insider Report*. It follows the activities of corporate insiders and other big shareholders. *Vickers* usually reports on companies not followed by Wall Street analysts. Discovering such little nuggets that could be potential takeover targets requires some work, of course. Investors need to take the time to browse through the lists of insiders in *Vickers* or other sources. The names often lead to profitable ideas that you would not have known otherwise.

One of the companies that produced big returns was discovered by LaLoggia from scanning the *Vickers* list. The company was Brylane Inc., a major U.S. catalogue retailer that also publishes catalogues for major companies like Sears, Lane Bryant, Lerner, and Chadwick's. An early investor in the initial public offering was Pinault-Printemps-Redoute, a major French retailer, which acquired a 43.7 percent stake. *Vickers* reported that in 1998, Pinault went to the open market and bought more shares. What prompted the increased buying was the huge drop in the stock, by 11 points to $24 a share. The reason for the drop: Brylane's Lerner catalog disappointed expectations. Brylane responded by buying back some $40 million worth of its shares. It's a classic example of a company buying back its shares after other investors panicked and bailed out.

Even so, the Brylane stock continued to fall, to $14 a share. One odd thing was that although Pinault steadily continued buying shares, the stock kept going down. Once again, Pinualt went to the open market and bought some more, lifting its stake to 47 percent. That prompted Brylane to pin down Pinault into signing a three-year standstill agreement through April 3, 2001, to keep its stake at that level. Pinault's annual revenues at the time totaled $4.5 billion, so it had the wherewithal to buy Brylane outright, whose market cap was about $300 million. In November 1998, the stock continued to slide, hitting a low of $10 a share, following another warning from the company that earnings were not looking good.

Several weeks later, the Brylane stock surprised everyone by driving up from $11 to $23 a share. The reason: Pinault finally made a buyout bid for Brylane. Investors who had the courage to buy the stock at $14 a share obviously hit a home run with Brylane. LaLoggia was one of those who hit the ball over the fence, crediting *Vickers*, where he first noticed how the name Brylane appeared again and again as insiders continued to buy shares. He had never heard of either Brylane or Pinault until he saw the names repeatedly mentioned in the *Vickers* report.

For any astute investor, it was easy to see how Brylane could end up as a takeover target, particularly because of the fact that insiders like Pinault continued to buy shares in the open market. You would think that buying a stock like Brylane, which had plummeted from $60 to $14 a share, would be like catching a falling piano. Some people might have thought so, but it didn't turn out that way at all. It was a great takeover catch.

Of course, it is always more comfortable for investors to buy large-cap stocks like General Electric Co. or International Business Machines Inc., shares of which almost everybody owns. But the biggest rewards come from stocks that are little known. You have to be prepared, of course, to face risks, such as volatility, inadequate information, and lack of trading volume. Large-cap stocks don't see much of a see-saw pattern. They trade fairly evenly; some call that **safe** or **low-risk investing**. And information about the large-caps abounds. However, neither do large-caps see sharp upward swings, as the small-cap stocks do on occasion. The thing to remember is that the bigger the risks, the bigger the rewards.

In the next chapter, we explore the idea of embracing undiscovered and unheard-of stocks in both the U.S. and foreign markets. The maxim Don't Fear the Unknown in Chapter 6 will demonstrate that even in some unfamiliar grounds, certain risk-laden stocks could turn out to be valuable gems.

COMMANDMENT 6

Don't Fear the Unknown

"The only thing we have to fear is fear itself."

—Franklin Delano Roosevelt, in his first inaugural address, on March 4, 1933

"To conquer fear is the beginning of wisdom."

—Bertrand Russell, 1950

This chapter deals with what most investors fear: the unknown. The truth of the adage that "the stock market hates uncertainty" was driven home in the second half of 2007 when the problems in the subprime mortgage market infected the entire credit spectrum and sent stock prices tumbling. Indeed, the plunge in the prices of U.S. mortgage-based securities shook the global financial markets.

But let's not forget that such waves of uncertainty and fear are inherent in the stock market. We have had market crashes galore in the past 35 years. Take, for example, the dark clouds of gloom that engulfed the market in the aftermath of the oil embargo in 1973, the double-digit rise in interest rates in 1987, the Russian debt default in 1988, the dot-com bubble burst in 2000, and the horrific September 11, 2001 terrorist attacks. Where did the market go after those nightmarish events? In each case, the market rectified itself and moved higher—to record levels.

This chapter's commandment, Don't Fear the Unknown, homes in on two areas of stock investing—foreign markets and biotechnology—that offer outsized returns but, because of a lack of understanding of their potential, perennially turn off investors. I explain why people are confused about these markets and suggest how you can profit from the confusion.

The Far-Flung Markets

Let us first address the mystery of the faraway markets. The foreign stock markets are among the most misunderstood and hardest to fathom. Yet foreign stocks have become very attractive and have delivered super gains, in part because of the force of globalization, which has unleashed tremendous liquidity into the markets, and investors' unabated hunger for golden opportunities. Some of the concerns about putting one's money in foreign stocks are valid but, as we shall soon see, they are overrated.

Surely, the unknown is always worrisome, but getting to know what's behind it, and learning how to understand its merits, will prove rewarding.

Investing in stocks involves all kinds of risks. There is no risk-free type of investing, except possibly in government bonds. But here, too, there are risks: When inflation ratchets up, interest rates climb and bond prices fall.

People assign too high a risk premium to certain investments because of fear of what they don't know in foreign markets. But these areas are far less risky than you would think, and the rewards are well worth the risks. The first advice from professionals who specialize in foreign market investing: Don't be intimidated.

A major rule in investing in foreign markets is to inform yourself about the foreign country's economic system and political structure.

It is the best way to know the range of risks and rewards you have to deal with. When it comes to investing in the emerging economies—in countries like China, India, Brazil, and even Russia, which has emerged from a communist system to a market-oriented economy—make sure you go for companies that are easy to understand.

It is far easier, and it creates less anxiety, when you invest in developed foreign markets, like the United Kingdom, as compared to putting money in, say, Brazil. Buying shares in British Petroleum is a lot less risky than buying shares in Brazil's Companhia de Bebidas, its major beverage company. But the rewards in undeveloped markets may be a lot greater.

Here is my own observation of investing in foreign markets: Emerging markets over the long run will pay off far more handsomely than buying stocks in the industrially developed world.

The emerging markets were the big winners in 2006 and 2007; they outpaced by a wide margin the U.S. market indexes. That was not a fluke. They also beat U.S. stocks in 2003, 2004, and 2005, and they are likely to outperform in 2008.

Fueling most of the interest in the overseas markets is China. According to Joseph Quinlan, chief market strategist of Global Wealth and Investment Management at Bank of America, U.S. investor purchases of Chinese stocks soared to $49 billion in 2005. And in 2006, U.S. investors' buying increased to $54 billion. That represents a transformation from prior years. U.S. investors owned few Chinese stocks prior to 2004 because of concern that the risks were too much to handle and that regulations were too stifling. And opportunities at the time seemed limited.

Not anymore. China has become the key emerging market for U.S. investors, representing 12.7 percent of total purchases by U.S. investors in 2005 and 10 percent more in 2006. It was a lot more in 2007. China's benchmark index has quadrupled in value in less than two years, and it soared 165.7 percent in 2007.

China's Booming Market

The Shanghai stock market eased somewhat in the latter half of 2007, but was still at an all-time high of 6,124 on October 16, 2007. To show you the extent of what it has done, by December 31, 2007, not only did Shanghai climb 165.7 percent, but Hong Kong also advanced, by 39.3 percent.

Some market observers worry that the advance by the Chinese markets is a bubble waiting to burst. In the meantime, however, Chinese investors, led mostly by greenhorn amateur individual investors, have continued to buy, buy, buy, with no let-up in sight.

It is possible that the Chinese markets will experience a sharp decline, as we witnessed in February 2007. But the market rebound thereafter was equally sharp and robust. We must remember that most stock markets are rocked by jolts of volatility periodically, and so will China's. Because China's markets are just starting to take off, they have yet to blossom fully, before experiencing the hard lessons they have yet to learn.

In the meantime, China's markets will do what the U.S. markets and others have done—grow and flourish. In time, the Chinese investors will learn the importance of looking at fundamentals, such as corporate earnings, price-earnings ratios, and growth prospects.

The entire emerging markets have also performed superbly. As measured by the Morgan Stanley Capital Index, they soared 41 percent at year-end 2006, from its low in mid-June 2006. Those results far outpaced the 19.3 percent advance by the Dow Jones Industrial Average and the 18.9 percent rise of S&P 500 stock index. The NASDAQ during the same period gained 20.5 percent.

The emerging markets have galloped in four years, since the global market rally started in 2002 through year-end 2006, achieving cumulative returns of nearly 270 percent. That was well ahead of the cumulative returns of the NASDAQ (115 percent), S&P 500 (80 percent), and the Dow (70.6 percent).

The Standard & Poor's observed that in the second quarter of 2007, returns from the world's emerging markets again outpaced that of the developed markets. Emerging equity markets climbed 14.81 percent in the second quarter, versus 6.82 percent for developed markets. In the past 12 months ending June 2007, the emerging stock markets posted a 49.8 percent return, twice the 24.4 percent gain by developed markets. India posted a 66 percent gain in 2006. South Africa, whose equity returns of 39 percent made it an enticing market, was also among the big gainers. Other emerging markets that provided hefty returns included Russia, Chile, Poland, and Brazil.

The markets in the emerging countries will continue to be in high gear. Why? For one thing, gross domestic growth in these countries is accelerating. In China, for example, growth in 2007 approached 12 percent, up from 2006's 11 percent—about four times the GDP growth in the United States. China is industrializing, and its rising young population is earning more money than it ever did before.

Demographic growth is one big factor to consider when picking stocks in these countries. Large young populations tend to drive consumer demand in the emerging countries. As these people go through various phases in their lives, demand for consumer goods begins to ramp up.

There are ways to play these changes in places like India, Turkey, Brazil, Poland, Russia, and Southeast Asia. Opportunities are created in a country that's in the process of transitioning from the old to the new, more modern, westernized type of lifestyle. Examples are the popularization of cell phones, wider Internet access, and the spread of banking services. These changes greatly improve business conditions. In these transitional periods, new companies are created to accommodate the increasing demand from consumers of products such as cell phones, computers, credit cards, and banking ATM machines.

The bottom line: Companies that cater to these new developments like wireless phone companies, computer makers and distributors, and banks are good investment opportunities.

Not surprisingly, U.S. institutional investors have been the big players in these remote markets. The emerging markets are a playground where these investors dare to be adventurous because they have the capabilities and resources to figure out what's going on. They scour these markets because technology has made it easier to monitor and keep in touch with companies abroad. Because most individual investors don't know much about foreign markets, the institutions have been able to establish footholds ahead of most everyone. After they have secured their portfolios with their foreign gems, they let the rest of the world know the allure of foreign stocks.

Cutting in on Undervalued Stocks

Individual investors can cut in and catch the play in some of these undervalued foreign stocks. But buying directly on local stock exchanges is not recommended. In the first place, it isn't easy to open personal trading accounts in foreign countries—even through your broker, unless he is thoroughly learned and a well-connected professional in the countries where you want to invest. Some countries, such as China, don't even allow foreigners to establish accounts. Even if an investor were able to open an account, some basic problems could be burdensome, such as dealing with complex tax implications, currency fluctuations, accounting methods, and trading rules.

Another worry is not being able to remit profits to your local bank back home. Of late, the transfer of money to and from overseas has become a big issue. Since the passage of the Patriot Act, banks have been required to be on the lookout for suspicious money transfers.

How then do you invest in the overseas markets? A variety of methods are available to investors, but the simplest is to buy mutual funds that invest in foreign markets. Another pathway is Exchange Traded Funds, or ETFs, which hold portfolios of stocks of companies in different countries all over the globe. The third option is American

Depository Receipts, or ADRs, which are certificates with all the characteristics of a stock that represent ownership in foreign corporations.

You must decide which of these avenues is best, based on the investor's risk tolerance and patience to deal with the different aspects of each investing vehicle.

Mutual Funds

Practically every major mutual fund company runs international or global funds, including Fidelity, Dimensional Funds, JPMorgan Chase, Janus, Morgan Stanley, Franklin Templeton, and Vanguard. Some of these companies have funds specifically tailored to the emerging markets, such as Vanguard, Fidelity, and Dimensional Funds. You can invest in these mutual funds like other domestic mutual funds, through your broker, local bank, or directly from the mutual fund company. You have a vast array of mutual funds to choose from. Among the international funds, Dan Wiener, editor of AdviserOnline.com, the independent adviser for Vanguard Investors, recommends Vanguard Global Equity Fund (VHGEX), which posted a return of 11 percent in 2007; Vanguard International Value Fund, up 12.7 percent; and Vanguard International Explorers (VINEX), up 5.2 percent.

Most of the international mutual funds bask in glory compared to the performance of domestic-type funds. For instance, Fidelity's Southeast Asian Fund posted a whopping 55.4 percent return in 2007; its Emerging Market Fund turned in 45.1 percent; and its Latin American Fund gained 43.7 percent. In comparison, Fidelity's domestic funds, such as the once-legendary Magellan Fund, posted a paltry 18.8 gain, and Fidelity's Aggressive Growth Fund registered a 18.8 percent gain. Dimensional Fund's Emerging Markets Fund was also hot, posting a hefty 30.5 percent return. And Vanguard's Emerging Market Fund scored a gain of 38.9 percent, beating the S&P Index Fund's 3.5 percent.

What is the secret driver behind the sharp advance of the international mutual funds? One big factor is globalization and the rise in the number of investors overseas, plus the jump in interest among U.S. investors in foreign stocks.

As the U.S. markets posted record highs in early 2007, more U.S. investors started to shift their focus to the international markets. And let us face it: Stocks in the foreign markets are something new and exciting to U.S. investors, particularly institutional investors who are always scouting around for new areas to invest in to rope in potential winners. They have ample resources to jump at every opportunity worldwide in a big way, and invest heavily in these markets that they regard as still very much undervalued.

Exchange Traded Funds (ETFs)

Exchange Traded Funds, or ETFs, are another convenient way of participating in funds that invest practically everywhere in the world. ETFs have become vastly popular because many of them deliver astounding returns.

What are they? ETFs are set up to trade a bundle of stocks. They resemble index mutual funds, but ETFs trade on exchanges as a single stock. In the past five years, there has been a flood of ETFs in the market, trading millions of shares every trading session. Their rising popularity is due to the simplicity they bring to investors: You can buy ETFs on almost every sector or industry or country.

In the foreign markets, ETFs concentrate on specific countries. If, for example, you believe South Korea would be a winner (symbol EWY), you would have been absolutely on the money: It gained 31 percent in 2007. Brazil (EWZ) posted a 72.3 percent gain, and Malaysia (EWM), 39.9 percent. When you compare those gains to France's (EWQ) 11.1 percent, Japan's –6.5 percent, and the United Kingdom's 2.9 percent, you will get the picture and understand the difference between the returns of developed and underdeveloped or emerging countries. Germany is an exception among the big countries: It posted a 31.8 percent gain. ETF portfolios now have more than $460 billion in assets, up about 50 percent at the end of 2005.

One staunch advocate of ETFs, Joseph Battipaglia, chief investment officer of Washington Crossing Advisors (an affiliate of investment bank Ryan Beck & Co.), prefers ETFs over investing in index mutual funds, mainly because of the cost advantage and trading flexibility. ETFs are cheaper to buy than index mutual funds, which strive to outperform such major market indexes as the S&P 500. That's because ETFs benefit from low management expenses. On average, ETFs have a large expense advantage because they are able to save money on many administrative costs. Mutual fund operations are comparably more costly. ETFs are faster to execute, too, he says, because they offer trading flexibility. ETF investors can buy or sell their shares without limit throughout the trading session, and they are priced continuously like stocks. Thus, an investor knows the price of an ETF at the time of the trade. A mutual fund, on the other hand, can be bought only at its net asset value at the close of the session. Hence, investors have been getting the positive message about ETFs versus mutual funds. Huge amounts of cash have continued to flow into ETFs. To illustrate, iShares Emerging Markets Index (EEM) received an inflow of more than $15 billion during an eight-week period in early 2007, versus the $700 million intake of open-end mutual funds that invest in emerging markets.

Among foreign ETFs, Battipaglia favors the MSCI (Morgan Stanley Capital Index) ETF called EAFE, trading with the symbol EFA. It is a basket of 800 stocks in Europe, Australia, and parts of Asia, including Japan. (In the U.S., the most popular ETF is the S&P's SPDRs, which holds shares representing the S&P 500 stock index.) Other favored buys among the foreign ETFs include those that represent assets in such foreign countries as Japan (EWJ), South Korea (EWY), Belgium (EWK), Brazil (EWZ), and Hong Kong (EWH).

Michael Metz, a veteran value investor and money manager who is the chief market strategist at Oppenheimer & Co., recommends taking advantage of the booming growth in the Pacific Rim of Asia. He recommends buying a broad ETF—specifically Vanguard's Pacific ETF (VPL), which trades on the American Stock Exchange, rather than picking an individual stock as a vehicle. AdviserOnline.com's Dan Wiener favors Vanguard's Emerging Markets ETF (VWO), which is up 34.8 percent in 2007. Its portfolio includes big and small stocks in emerging countries, including Mexico's Cemex, Taiwan's Cathay Financial Holdings, Brazil's Petroleo Braziliero, India's Infosys Technologies, South Africa's Sasol Ltd., and Hong Kong's PetroChina.

The advice that you should inform yourself about a country's economy and political situation applies to ETFs in spades. The South Korean ETF, for example, is attractive because of the country's relatively stable economy that has been in a growth mode. Korea has spawned an array of technology companies, which have grown to become global producers of important products, such as television sets, wireless phones, and cars. Hugely significant is the improving political situation in the country. The country's relationship with communist North Korea, for one, has grown closer and warmer.

On the other hand, Venezuela is not such a hot pick these days because of what's happening there, with Venezuelan President Hugo Chavez trying to nationalize or seize practically every foreign company in the country.

How should an individual investor not conversant with foreign markets or emerging countries invest in ETFs? Investing in them requires the same amount of diligent homework needed to invest in individual stocks. The same adage applies: The more you know, the better your chances of making money.

The first step is familiarization. Read up as much as you can about ETFs, which are widely covered by many major newspaper publications and magazines, as well as their online versions, including

The Wall Street Journal and the weekly Barron's. The *Journal* lists the ETFs names, trading symbols, and prices and price changes. Many Web sites also provide information about ETFs, such as AdviserOnline.com, Yahoo.com, Charles Schwab, and the S&P.

In addition, various newsletters provide information on ETFs. One good source of information is MorningStar, an independent research company. In addition to providing data and information on stocks and the market, it publishes all kinds of data and a sourcebook on ETFs. The publication provides tips on how to analyze ETFs and how to best monitor their performance. By looking at the facts and data, you get a feel of how certain ETFs behave. You can track an ETF's trading history and get to know how much it has gained or lost during a certain period.

Some say investing in ETFs is a cakewalk, a lot easier than picking stocks. Not necessarily. There are as many basics to learn about ETFs as there are to know about stocks. There is no substitute for a hard examination of facts and figures.

Perhaps the best way to wet your feet in ETFs is to experiment with one or two ETFs. Invest and see how it goes. You don't have to track them every day; just watch them on weekly basis. That is the most practical way of dipping in the tempting waters of investing. Start small and slow because, in that way, you will begin learning on your own the many aspects of investing. Equally important, you will get to know more about yourself, from the way you react to your initial venture. You might discover that you don't want to have anything to do with ETFs.

American Depositary Receipts (ADRs)

What are ADRs? An ADR is a form similar to a stock certificate registered in the holder's or investor's name. The certificate represents a number of shares in a foreign corporation. Companies with

ADRs comply with U.S. regulations and file the required documents just like any other U.S. company. The holder is entitled to all dividends and capital gains. Most ADRs trade on the New York Stock Exchange. One of their attractions is that they probably represent the least risk among foreign equities because they are usually large-cap stocks favored by the big institutions. Not that they are immune to market declines. But the added advantage is that the investor has access to basic information about the company's history and prospects. Based on readily available information, an investor has an easier time analyzing a company. If you are a long-term stock picker, the ADRs will suit you best.

Let's take a close look at some interesting ADRs in four emerging markets that aren't well known to U.S. investors but have performed well—and continue to look quite attractive.

In Brazil, Companhia de Bebidas Americas has been a standout performer. A beer and beverage producer, it is one of the largest in Latin America, trading with the ADR symbol ABV. Apart from beer (its top seller is Stella Artois beer), the company produces soft drinks, tea, mineral water, juices, and sports drinks. It has run up from $38 per ADR in July 2006 to $71.03 on December 31, 2007. The ADR's strong performance is driven by the company's earnings growth. It is the type of beverage maker that Anheuser-Busch, the number-one U.S. brewer, might one day decide to take an active interest in. Bebidas is the licensed distributor of Pepsi Cola in Brazil. Among the bulls on Bebidas are Citigroup, Bear Stearns, and JPMorgan Chase.

In Turkey, Turkcell Iletisim Hizmet AS is the dominant mobile phone company, with a 62.5 percent market share. Trading with the ticker symbol TKC, Turkcell tripled from $9 in July 2006 to $27.57 on December 31, 2007. The company has extended its reach to other countries, including Azerbaijan, Kazakhstan, Georgia, Northern Cyprus, and Moldova. It also owns a major stake in a phone company in Ukraine. Analysts expect it to post whopping profits of $1.1 billion in 2008 on sales of $5.1 billion, up from an estimated $1 billion in

2007 on sales of $4.8 billion. Turkcell made $854 million on sales of $4.6 billion.

In India, one highly favored ADR is Tata Motors, the country's leading vehicle manufacturer, whose ADR trades on the New York Stock Exchange with the symbol TTM. It has climbed from $14 in July 2006 to $22 in early 2007, but it slipped to $18.86 by December 31, 2007. Established in 1954 to make steam locomotives, it formed a partnership in the same year with Daimler Benz to produce commercial vehicles. That alliance ended in 1969, and Tata has since expanded to manufacturing trucks, tankers, buses, and sport utility vehicles (SUVs). Sales have been on the rise, with commercial volume jumping 50 percent in 2006 and passenger vehicles rising by 27 percent. Analysts expect the big rise in sales to continue beyond 2007. One project on the horizon for Tata is its efforts to expand its car markets. It has made a bid to acquire Ford Motor's Jaguar and Land Rover units. Although some people speculate that it could win in the bidding for Ford's luxury auto units, its rivals are quite as aggressive in trying to buy Jaguar and Land Rover. One of its competitors is Mahindra & Mahindra Ltd., of Germany, which has submitted a bid jointly with Apollo Management LP. The other bidder is One Equity Partners, a unit of JPMorgan Chase & Co. Among the bulls on Tata are Standard & Poor's Corp. and Matrix USA.

In China, one of the fastest growing businesses that appeals to the country's youth is online games. CDC Corp. is the pioneer in online games in China, trading on the NASDAQ with the symbol CHINA. Its stock has inched up from $4 a share in July 2006 to $4.87 a share on December 31, 2007. Another big Chinese play in online games is Shanda Interactive Entertainment, with the symbol SNDA. It is China's largest developer and operator of online games. Its stock, also trading on the NASDAQ, has rocketed from $13 a share in October 2006 to $33.34 a share on December 31, 2007. The online games don't involve gambling. Played over the Internet, multiple players participate as characters in virtual nations and engage in fantasy lives.

In Shanda's games, participants play for free and are charged only for the costumes or equipment created for the games. The characters that the players assume require special costumes and a variety of weapons and tools that Shanda makes and sells for the games.

These online role-playing games are widely popular in China and attract participants from other countries through the Internet. The players form teams to engage other groups in science-fiction type games or battles, mostly based on local stories and Chinese folklore. About 40 million Chinese play the games regularly, according to market research firm DFC Intelligence. In 2006, the games generated total revenues of $1 billion in China. Revenues in 2007 significantly exceeded $1 billion.

Tian X. Hou, managing director at Pali Research in New York and a specialist in Chinese stocks, describes Shanda as the "best pure play investment in China's online action-gaming industry." She predicts Shanda's sales will rocket to $100 million by 2008 from 2006's $44 million. Part of the jump is being driven by "in-game" online advertisements, a new source of revenues, says Hou. She figures the stock could hit $46 by 2008.

The Biotechs

Let's go back to the U.S. market, specifically to the mysterious biotechnology stocks. Biotech companies tend to intimidate investors. These are companies that are on the forefront of innovation in producing cures for a host of ailments that affect society—AIDS/HIV, Alzheimer's, cancer in all its forms, cystic fibrosis, diabetes, congestive heart failure, leukemia, multiple sclerosis, and schizophrenia. Except for a few giants like Genentech and Amgen, most of the biotech companies have yet to produce proven drugs and make money. Analysts usually turn off investors to these stocks because few of them are versed well enough to explain the attraction of the group. And biotechs are the moving targets of the short sellers, who persistently predict their downfall because they expect them to run out of money before they get FDA approval for their new drugs. But because they are the source of promising drugs, many of them end up being gobbled by the major drugmakers.

Big drugmakers initially try to partner with young biotechs to get early licensing commitments for their drugs even before they are launched. The promise of new drugs and partnerships—if not outright buyout attempts by the major drugmakers—represent the most valuable assets of the biotechs.

During periods when the biotechs are hard at work testing and developing their products, they are usually ignored by investors. With the unappetizing combination of still-unproved products and limited market capitalization, the biotechs command little respect—until they get close to launching a new drug. By that time, however, the price of the biotech's stock has already doubled, if not tripled. I see this happen often, where the major drugmakers—and investors—end up paying a steep price for biotechs because they waited too long to come up to the plate.

A perfect example of this was Isis Pharmaceuticals (ISIS). Few paid attention to this young biotech, but I wrote about it in my "Inside Wall Street" column on November 27, 2006. I wrote that Isis was a name to watch in the lucrative area of cholesterol reduction. It had released favorable data two weeks before at the American Heart Association in Chicago, which showed that a cholesterol-lowering drug it was developing cut the levels of bad cholesterol by 62 percent in patients who took it for three months. The stock was then trading at $10 a share. Guess what? On January 8, 2008, Genzyme (GENZ), a pharmaceutical company, partnered with Isis to develop the drug and agreed to pay $1.9 billion. The stock of Isis jumped that day to $18.58, from $14 the day before. Obviously, people who bought the stock at $10 after I recommended Isis in my column made good money on the stock.

The key to putting your money in a biotech—and being able to sleep at night—is to balance the risks against the rewards. So what is an individual investor to do? Once again, do the homework. There is no shortcut to success, especially in biotech investing. The good thing, though, is that the Internet is brimming with information about companies, including biotechs. The first step is to determine which company or biotech you would like to know about and invest in. By reading periodicals and business publications, including *The Wall Street Journal, BusinessWeek, Fortune, Barron's, Forbes, The New York Times, Money*, and their Internet counterparts, as well as newswire outlets like Bloomberg and Reuters, investors will come across worthy articles about biotechs.

After you have picked a name, go to the company's Web site, or use Google or the Yahoo Finance page to get the company's corporate profile. Companies adhere to the government's requirement on Regulation FD (full disclosure) by making public general information about themselves. So, in compliance, the companies disclose information via the Internet or in document filings with the SEC. They also provide fact sheets on request about their background and operations, technology, and science.

These fact sheets can be helpful to investors hoping to know a company's specific product pipelines. Also, investors should look at corporate presentations to Wall Street analysts or institutional investors, which are usually reported on a company's Web site. They are vital sources of information, particularly the question-and-answer period in such presentations. It is helpful for investors to listen in on these question-and-answer sessions between the company's officials and Wall Street analysts. Companies provide webcasting or video presentations of these conferences, too, which are available on request.

Other sources generate data on practically all publicly traded companies. One popular outlet is the Web site www.EDGAR-Online.com, through which publicly traded U.S. companies release their annual statements of accounts, called Form 10-K, and their quarterly statements of accounts, called Form 10-Q. Materially important events are reported on Form 8-K, which typically includes all the company's press releases. This site also provides other filings, such as ownership of stocks, in Form 4s and 13Ds. These filings show how many shares management owns and whether they are buying or selling. *BusinessWeek* Online has a particularly valuable source of data, called the Company Insight Center, which lets you dig into data on more than 350,000 companies—public and private—worldwide. It is one of the best, if not *the* best, company resource on the free Web. Just log on at http://investing.businessweek.com/research/company/overview/overview.asp.

Investment research is also provided by investment banks, including the small regional- or retail (public)-oriented outfits. They often provide good information on various companies, including the competitive landscape in the industries they operate in. And then there are some advocacy groups and national organizations whose Web sites contain essential information. For example, if you are doing research on a company that has a specific drug targeting a specific disease, say breast cancer, you could search its Web site and find articles that discuss the company's pertinent therapeutic strategies, including currently approved treatments. You will also find the latest drugs or therapies in the making for specific diseases. After going through all these information outlets, an investor should feel quite informed about specific companies and their products or drugs in development.

Even the big institutional investors go through this kind of basic research process to learn about specific companies. After they have done that, their research staff members scope out specifics dictated by their particular strategies. One major reason why investors go for biotechs in spite of the risks and their complexity is the prospect of reaping gigantic profits. However, biotechs are best when you take a long-term view. It takes many years for a small outfit to come up with products that work. Many biotechs don't make it that far. But when they do, the long-awaited jackpot is worth the wait. Sometimes the waiting period doesn't take too long. Some investors pick the right biotech at the right time, and given the right management, product, and luck, these companies hit the jackpot within a relatively short period.

How the Pros Check Out the Biotechs

Let us take a close look at how some big players, such as hedge funds, do basic research. Peeking into how they do it will show individual investors the process of how they analyze these complex biotechs.

One such investor is SCO Financial Group, which manages assets for long-term clients, including several hedge funds. A value investor, SCO focuses on little-known biotechs. After its portfolio managers or stock pickers decide on a company they want to invest in—after they have done basic research as I have described—other factors come into play.

SCO encounters a lot of arcane situations because it invests only in small-cap stocks—those with market caps of $100 million to $250 million. So how does SCO decide which companies are worth buying?

SCO President Jeffrey Davis picks companies with multiple products in development, or technology platforms from which product candidates can be developed. SCO discards single-product companies because failure in that one product could doom the company. The next step is to look for companies whose lead products have been tested in at least one or more clinical trials and have shown to be effective in humans.

For the novice, when a company says a product is in preclinicals, it means the product is being tested in petri dishes or animal models (like mice). Well, lots of things kill cancer in mice but fail in humans. Phase I trials are the first stage of human clinical trials. Such tests only look at safety, not drug activity or efficacy. Lots of things are safe but aren't necessarily active or effective. Phase II and Phase III trials are the human clinical trials that test for drug activity and efficacy. What you look for is whether the products have shown signs of activity and efficacy in humans. If a company is worth researching further, SCO taps its own network of health care professionals, clinicians, and corporate executives to find new opportunities.

Scrutinize the Managers

The next thing SCO scrutinizes is management. Surely this is not easy to divine for the individual investor. But SCO explains some basic pointers. One way it judges management is by looking at how successful the company's top officers have been in their past jobs or ventures. Obviously, the most important person to scrutinize is the CEO and his close aides—the chairman, chief financial officer, and chief operating officer. Individual investors can check the history of their corporate lives, which is usually laid out in a company's annual report. It is important to find out how successful managers were in raising funds in the companies they served previously, and how productive they were in drug development. How successful were managers in getting partnerships or creating shareholder value? Their successes or failures are a more important gauge than whether they obtained PhDs from Ivy League universities. Success breeds success, and the men or women who have done it before can, surely, be expected to do it again.

It is important to have patience while doing research. Drugs take years or even decades to develop, and often it takes years for the real value of a product to be recognized. This is why SCO's average holding period in a stock exceeds 18 months, sometimes longer. However, the payoff is great. SCO's returns are "super-normal," says Davis, far exceeding the performance of both the broader market indices and popular biotech averages, because of the time he and his staff devote to research.

Calculating the value of a biotech company that has yet to make money is difficult, especially for the individual investor. The method that is commonly followed by Wall Street is to use the discounted earnings model, in which the analyst predicts the size of the market (for a particular product) and the estimated market share to gauge a potential drug candidate's future sales. Then the analyst uses a discount rate based on the product's chances of being marketed commercially.

There are other factors to consider. One is the drug candidate's stage of development and who its competitors are.

John McCamant, editor of *The Medical Technology Stock Letter*, says he uses this method of evaluating biotechs to some extent. But sometimes a company's inherent value may be better understood, he argues, by using a sum-of-the-parts valuation in which you put a value on the separate components on an individual basis and then add the sums together to arrive at a company's total value. "We have used this method in the past when we first evaluated during its [the company's] infancy, and we believe that it can provide a useful perspective for investors," says McCamant.

Biotech ETFs

You might not have the capacity to do this kind of sum-of-the-parts valuation, but it is good to know how the pros do it as a guide. If you have no inclination to do this type of painstaking research, ETFs might come to the rescue. There are ETFs devoted to investing in biotechs. One of them is iShares NASD Biotech Index, whose ticker symbol is IBB and which traded at $81 a share on December 31, 2007. Managed by Barclays Global Fund Advisors, this ETF owns shares in a host of large-cap and small-cap biotechs, including

Amgen, Gilead Sciences, Biogen Idec, and Illumina. Another ETF in biotechs is PowerShares Dynamic Biotechnology & Genome Portfolio, with the symbol PBE, which traded at $18 a share on December 31, 2007. Managed by PowerShares Capital Management, this ETF owns shares in Applera, Genzyme, Genentech, Dendreon, Amgen, Sigma-Aldrich, and Isis Pharmaceuticals.

Let's look at several little-known biotechs that have outscored their peers and how investors discovered them, which could be helpful to the novice investor.

Advanced Neuromodulation Systems (ANSI)

Advanced Neuromodulation Systems is in the business of managing chronic pain. What's neuromodulation? It is the delivery of electrical stimulation to nerve fibers to ease pain. The company has developed an implantable pulse generator system that stimulates the spinal cord to remedy intractable chronic pain. The company's stock itself was in great pain: It plunged from $47 a share in February 2004 to $27 on May 12, 2004. The entry of another company, Advanced Bionics, into the pain control business prompted many investors in Neuromodulation Systems to bail out. However, some smart-money pros took the decline as an opportunity. Peggy Farley, president of Ascent Capital Management, was one of them. Because there were only a handful of players in the field, Farley felt the company could end up as a buyout target of Big Pharma. There were rumors that Johnson & Johnson was looking to broaden its stake in the nueromodulation market, which was then dominated by Medtronic. Other factors provided allure to the stock. Some clinicians believed that neuromodulation had potential in treating other major ailments, such as Alzheimer's and depression.

Neuromodulation Systems did get bought out, but Johnson & Johnson wasn't the buyer. St. Jude Medical bought the company in 2005 for $62 a share. Neuromodulation Systems wasn't a well-known stock but, like many biotechs, its value was in the potential worth of its products. St. Jude recognized that it needed to be in that field more broadly.

Cleveland BioLabs (CBLI)

Cleveland BioLabs, which went public in July 2006 at $6 a share, started off fast and has since been running faster. It obtained exclusive rights from the Cleveland Clinic Foundation, famous for treating heart ailments and cancer, for its cancer and molecular genetic technology. So far, BioLabs has produced two drugs: Curaxins, now in Phase III clinical trials, aimed at prostate and renal cancer; and Protectan, a treatment for exposure to severe levels of radiation. Its funding came mainly from various government grants, including $9 million from the National Institutes of Health, the Defense Department, and NASA. And it expects to receive a contract from the Defense Department for its radiation protection compound, Protectan, which has the ability to mitigate damaging effects of ionizing radiation on the gastrointestinal system. Protectan has also shown significant survival benefits that comply with the Defense Department's requirements. Some investors expect BioLabs first contract from the Pentagon to go as high as $200 million, based on similar awards in the past. Protectan has demonstrated effectiveness against radiation when applied two hours prior to exposure or up to eight hours after.

One early investor in Cleveland Biolabs was Cynthia Ekberg Tsai, general partner at Madelin Fund, who says BioLabs is a stock to invest in because, for the first time, Cleveland Clinic can commercialize its advanced and innovative technology for cancer and tissue protection through BioLabs. She bought the stock at around $4 a share in September 2006. By September 12, 2007, the stock had catapulted to $13.68. Investors who missed buying shares when the stock was trading at $4 got another chance to buy the stock at an even lower price. The stock plunged on January 4, 2008, to $3.31 a share, when the Department of Defense awarded a $225 million contract to a rival of Cleveland Biotech—the very contract that Cleveland Biotech was vying for. CEO Michael Fonstein said Cleveland Biotech has had positive meetings with the Department of Defense over Protectan and had expected to win the contract. He said the company will continue developing Protectan and will persist in seeking to win a contract from the Department of Defense.

MedImmune (MEDI)

MedImmune was another one of the biotechs that ended up in the arms of Big Pharma. MedImmune is a major maker of the influenza vaccine, Flu-Mist. It got into big trouble in 2004 when sales of its spray vaccine failed to meet Wall Street's expectations. Its stock reeled, dropping from $42 in June 2003 to $23 on March 29, 2004.

Although it had another product, Synagis, a treatment for lower respiratory diseases in children and approved for pediatric congenital disease, MedImmune turned off a lot of investors. One who dared buy shares when nobody wanted them was David Katz, president of Matrix Asset Advisors. He was confident that MedImmune could turn its Flu-Mist business around by pricing it lower and educating physicians about the product. Another reason he liked it: Katz believed that with MedImmune shares so beleaguered, one of the Big Pharma companies would come knocking on its door to buy the company. Billionaire activist-investor Carl Icahn had the same idea, so he purchased some 4.1 million MedImmune shares. He badgered the company and pressured it to put itself on the block. As it turned out, at least one of the big drugmakers was paying attention. London-based AstraZeneca agreed in April 2005 to buy MedImmune for $15.1 billion, or $58 a share. Both Katz and Icahn did very well on MedImmune, along with some readers of my "Inside Wall Street" column, where I featured the company twice, once on March 29, 2004, when the stock was at $23 a share, and then again on January 15, 2007, when it was trading at $33. In both instances, I discussed the stock as buyout bait.

Some Unrecognized Attractive Biotechs

Let us take a look at several biotechs—some of them still unrecognized or with scant Wall Street following but whose prospects look tantalizing because of their huge potential value.

Enzo Biochem (ENZ)

Enzo Biochem, which trades on the New York Stock Exchange, is one of the oldest U.S. biotechs around. But it gets little attention from Wall Street. One reason: It hasn't approached the major investment banks for financial help. It has managed to coast along without doing even a secondary public offering since it went public in June 1980 at split-adjusted $6.25 a share. What's unusual about Enzo is its financial wherewithal, considering that it is a small company with a market cap of just $519 million. Biotechs are usually strapped for cash. Enzo, on the other hand, had $100 million in cash on its balance sheet during its fiscal third quarter of 2007, generated from product sales and lab fees, which make about $120 million a year. And cash flow from operations amounted to $200 million annually. In 2006, private equity financing provided Enzo with $65 million.

Enzo's stock on September 4, 2007 traded at $18. But that doesn't tell you the entire history of its stock activity. In 1999, its stock climbed to $40, which was a huge jump from where it was the previous year—at $14. But that wasn't even the stock's best move. In 2000, when the market went wild and crazy as stocks of all stripes surged on the crest of the Internet stocks' upswing—before the bubble burst—Enzo rocketed to an all-time high of $114.36. The stock was swept up by a rambunctious market that loved companies with any kind of technology kicked into its products. Enzo's technology focused on harnessing genetic processes to develop research tools, diagnostics, and therapeutics. Unfortunately, the stock's ascent to the $100s signaled Enzo's peak. When the dot-com bubble burst in late 2000, everything went to pot—fast. By 2001, Enzo's stock had plummeted to $30. The stock kept going lower each year thereafter and, by January 10, 2008, the stock had settled down at $11.63.

Although Enzo stock is back to about where it was nine years ago, the company is now bigger. It expanded and broadened its products under development whose progress toward commercialization has improved. Enzo President Barry Weiner decided in 2006 that the company had to be restructured to sharpen its focus on three fields: life sciences, therapeutics, and clinical laboratories. So the company created three units to pursue these markets. Its life sciences unit aims to maximize the use of its vast intellectual property (it has 200 patents and 200 more pending approval) and increase revenue growth by developing new products, forming partnerships, and making acquisitions. Its second unit, the therapeutics division, will accelerate clinical studies on treatments for Crohn's disease and nonalcoholic steatohepatitis, which are both in Phase II clinical trials, and to pursue Phase I and II trials for its StealthVector HGTV43 gene against HIV-1 infection. The vector is used to transfer three antisense genes, designed to interfere with the growth of the HIV-1 virus, into blood stem cells. Enzo's third unit, the clinical labs, provides routine as well as esoteric, or specialized, lab services for physicians. It is also adding to its menu specialized pathology assays, such as tumor identification studies, and is exploring the addition of molecular genetic assays.

Although Wall Street has ignored Enzo, it has quite a roster of big institutions in its stock. The biggest stakeholder is ClearBridge Advisors, which owns a 13 percent stake. JPMorgan Chase owns 4.1 percent, mutual fund giant Vanguard Group owns 2.4 percent, and Citigroup owns 1 percent. Why are these big investors in the stock? For starters, the stock is way down from its all-time high. And Enzo already generates revenues from the sale of products and lab fees, which isn't common among biotechs. Another thing: Once Enzo breaks into the black and starts making money, the stock should start revving up. And the company has products in the oven that could become big winners. Two things might happen that will validate and justify the big investors' faith in Enzo. It has four important lawsuits for patent infringement against Big Pharma, among them Roche and Affymetrix. Otis Bradley, a veteran analyst with Gilford Securities, says a win in just one of these lawsuits will catapult the stock to much higher levels, possibly in the high 30s. And, should Enzo announce positive data on any one of its products that are now in clinical trials, such as its StealthVector gene against HIV, that should also be favorable news and cause the stock to soar. Bradley has been in and out of Enzo's stock, taking advantage of its gyrations during the past nine years. "I know Enzo well, having been with the stock all these years," says Bradley. "What you need plenty of when investing in biotechs, I have learned, is patience."

Rosetta Genomics (ROSG)

Rosetta Genomics is in an emerging field in biotechnology that is creating new excitement: RNA interference, or RNAi. It involves a naturally occurring mechanism within cells for selectively silencing and regulating specific genes. Its discovery has been acknowledged as a major breakthrough. Its potential broad impact on medicine was recognized with the awarding of the 2006 Nobel Prize for Physiology or Medicine to Dr. Andrew Z. Fire and Dr. Craig C. Mello. Because many diseases are caused by a specific gene's "inappropriate" activity, the ability to silence or turn off genes selectively through RNAi helps accelerate understanding these genes and their related pathways.

Merck, recognizing the pivotal role that RNAi could play in medicine, acquired on December 31, 2006, Sirna Therapeutics, Inc., an early player in RNAi. Alnylam Phamaceuticals, Inc. (ALNY) is also developing therapeutics based on RNAi.

What is RNA? It stands for ribonucleic acid, which has a specific role in the production of proteins. Many of today's medical needs cannot effectively be addressed with small molecules or antibodies, the current major classes of drugs. So the discovery of RNAi has been welcomed as an important contribution to medicine. "We are in the midst of an enlightenment period in the public markets for companies with an RNAi-related focus," observes Andrew S. Fein, a biotech analyst at investment firm C. E. Unterberg, Towbin. Rosetta gives investors a chance to participate in the next generation of RNAi therapeutics.

Here is how it all works: Genetic information carried in the DNA of all cells is encoded with instructions to produce proteins that carry out the body's functions, including antibodies to support immune functions, and enzymes to digest food. The DNA information is translated into messages carried by RNA to assemble specific proteins under certain types of circumstances. Drs. Fire and Mello discovered that the instructions conveyed by messenger RNA could be stopped via a specific mechanism called RNAi. How? The RNA activates a process that "degrades" the messengered RNA molecules, which makes the message in the gene disappear. Thus, the protein is not made.

All cells contain the same set of genes in an organism. Genes are composed of chromosomes that are made of the deoxribonucleic acid of DNA, which is responsible for determining the characteristics inherited by all organisms. Genes direct the coding and creation of proteins, involving RNA in a process called transcription. Where does Rosetta come in? It is involved with RNAi in a novel way, as the leader in another aspect of RNAi—microRNA-based cancer diagnostics. Using its proprietary informatic technologies, Rosetta has been able to identify at least 50 percent of human microRNAs, which are produced by cells in response to "signal pathways."

Pamela Bassett, biotech analyst at Cantor Fitzgerald, says microRNAs are useful biomarkers, or indicators of disease. These microRNAs, the next-generation market-disruptive technology, will enable the development of new diagnostics. Bassett expects Rosetta Genomics to launch the world's first microRNA cancer diagnostic in the latter part of 2008. The product will be the first microRNA-based diagnostic to identify cancers whose origin isn't yet known. Bassett says Rosetta's microRNA technology will drive breakthroughs in diagnostics and therapeutics for treating cancer and infectious diseases. The company's pipeline includes five cancer diagnostics and one therapeutic program in partnership with Isis Pharmaceuticals. Bassett also expects Rosetta to enter into at least one alliance with a major pharmaceutical company by 2008. When this was being written, in late mid-November 2007, Rosetta's stock was trading on the NASDAQ at $5.62 a share, down from its high of $9.84 on March 2, 2007. On January 8, 2008, the stock closed at $6.18. Bassett expects the stock to more than double by 2009.

With Rosetta's complex science and technology, how does Bassett arrive at such a valuation? Her primary benchmarks for early-stage biotechs with business models based upon the use of an enabling platform technology are "technology value" and market capitalization. "We use a price/technology value-per-share multiple to characterize a group of companies with enabling technologies at various development stages to determine an average multiple," explains Bassett. Based on such an average, she figures that Rosetta, trading at 1.82 times her estimated "technology value" of $3.73 a share, is trading at a big discount to its peer group's average multiple. Rosetta is significantly undervalued, she argues, because its technology has an "established proof," and she expects Rosetta to rapidly generate a revenue base in cancer diagnostics. Rosetta's first product, called CUP, and future products will become the standard-of-care diagnostics, she believes. Many currently available diagnostic tests are based on identifying the level of a single protein or multiple proteins as an indication of disease. MicroRNA-based tests, on the other hand, identify the genes that regulate the proteins and give a more accurate diagnosis of diseases—and more information about them, such as tumor aggressiveness and risk of recurrence, explains Bassett.

Access Pharmaceuticals, Inc. (ACCP)

Access Pharmaceuticals, Inc., develops products for the treatment and supportive care of cancer patients. It got quick attention when word got out that its lead product, ProLindac, a novel platinum-based drug aimed at several oncology applications, could be a potential blockbuster drug. I wrote about Access in my column on February 12, 2007, when it was trading over-the-counter at $2.95 share. One of the early investors, Kevin Raidy of health care hedge fund H4 Capital, which owned close to five percent of the stock, described ProLindac as a drug that could produce a home run for Access. The drug is Access's lead oncology product, now in Phase II clinical study, aimed at retarding tumors to a greater extent than existing drugs do. ProLindac uses a safe, water-soluble polymer to increase efficacy by delivering more DACH platinum to the tumor. What is a "platinum" drug? There are several forms of platinum drugs. DACH platinum is a chemical form of platinum, which some scientists describe as more effective than other forms of platinum against colorectal cancer. The global market for platinum is estimated at $5 billion to $6 billion, of which roughly half is generated by a platinum drug called Eloxatin, owned by Sanofi Aventis. Currently, Eloxatin is the drug of choice for colorectal cancer. However, its patent expires shortly, and a generic version is expected to come up by then. There is a likelihood that Sanofi may want to license Access' Prolindac.

Access has run its Prolindac DACH platinum drug through tests in the National Institute of Cancer against other platinum drugs, including Eloxatin, says SCO President Jeffrey Davis. It "was never worse than any other platinum and, most importantly, it was 'markedly superior' to Eloxatin in roughly half of all tumor types."

H4 Capital's Raidy figures Access's stock is extraordinarily cheap because the company's second product, MuGard, had already been approved by the FDA. To Raidy, that removed any risk in the stock because the drug alone, he figured, was worth more than the stock's price at the time.

The week following the appearance of Access in my column, the stock zoomed to $10.26 a share. SCO Financial Group had acquired early on a 30 percent stake in Access. SCO Chairman and Chief Investment Officer Steve Rouhandeh is betting big on Access because he believes the stock could hit $30 in three years, in part because of Prolindac's potential commercial value.

One of ProLindac's other potential applications is for the treatment of refractory ovarian cancer, which is a $2.5 billion market. According to Rouhandeh, ProLindac's molecular design could potentially eliminate some of the toxic neurological side effects seen in currently marketed platinum-based drugs. Prolindac is also being tested for head-and-neck cancer as well as for colorectal cancer. Access's other product, MuGard, is a proprietary oral rinse product for oral mucositis, the debilitating side effect that afflicts more than 40 percent of cancer patients who are undergoing radiation and chemotherapy. That market is about $1.5 billon. Access added four new cancer compounds to its product pipeline in 2007 when it acquired Somanta Pharmaceuticals, Inc. The acquisition fills out Access's cancer drug pipeline. Somanta's four cancer drugs have "unique mechanism of action," according to Rouhandeh. Here is why: One of the drugs, called Angiolix, is a humanized monoclonal antibody that causes anti-angiogenesis (it stops the growth of blood vessels to the tumor), resulting in the death of cancerous cells. Angiolix's importance is that it is similar in its effects to Genentech's cancer drug Avastin. Another Somanta drug is Sodium Phenylbutyrate, which is already approved in the U.S. for the treatment of a rare pediatric disorder, so its safety profile is already familiar to the FDA. It is now being clinically tested for treatment of brain cancer in the U.S. There is also some data that the drug might be an effective therapy for certain blood cancers and other solid tumors. SCO Financial bought a large stake in Access as a long-term investment, but its product pipeline helped deliver a short-term bonanza in the interim. Such short-term gains could also be provoked by the entry of influential investors, like George Soros, into the stock. These high-charging investors tend to entice others to join in. A surprise, like a favorable FDA action about a drug in the making, could occur with little warning. Or the company might attract a suitor and end up being acquired. Although the stock has since come down from its high, SCO Financial has continued to hold the stock. Part of the decline was due to Access's acquisition of Somanta, which closed in late December 2007. That, plus the market's steep decline because of the subprime meltdown, drove the stock down, closing at $3.25 a share on December 31, 2007.

In recent years, a lot of the big pharmaceutical companies have been poaching in biotech's backyard, snapping up some young outfits that they think have one or two promising drugs in their labs. But to repeat what has been emphasized in this book, patience and adherence to long-term strategies produce the best results.

The final chapter of this book, Chapter 7, focuses on long-term investment ideas and discusses the merits of taking advantage of the opportunities in the stock market from a longer time perspective. Chapter 7's commandment Always Invest for the Long Term, is a valid golden rule because it has been tested and proven to be worth applying time and time again, ad infinitum. It is the essence of old-fashioned investing. Invest early in an idea, stay and wait for it to develop, and then reap the prized bounty. If you invest in the right stock at the appropriate time, there is no reason why you shouldn't be rewarded munificently for your patience and perseverance.

COMMANDMENT 7

Always Invest for the Long Term: Seven Stocks for the Next Seven Years

"If the job has been correctly done when a common stock is purchased, the time to sell it is—almost never."

—Philip Fisher, author of *Uncommon Stocks and Common Profits* (1958)

Philip Fisher, whose original thinking as an investment manager in the 1930s turned into classic principles that have attracted strong believers, including Warren Buffett, extols the virtues of long-term investing. He rejects the concept of short-term trading, arguing that "you can make a lot of money by investing in an outstanding enterprise and holding it for years as it becomes bigger and better." Almost certainly, he adds, the market price of your share will rise to reflect its higher intrinsic value.

The legendary Benjamin Graham, like Fisher, was also critical of short-term strategies. So, it was not surprising that he was aghast when he got firsthand information at a Wall Street conference (shortly after the 1973 to 1974 market crash) on how money managers played the investment game. "I could not comprehend how the management of money by institutions had degenerated from sound investment to this rat race of trying to get the highest possible returns in the shortest period," remarked Graham.

This chapter's commandment, Always Invest for the Long Term, zeroes in on those principles—pursuing shares of companies that will stand the test of time and produce much better returns over the long haul. Instant gratification is a tantalizing temptation, but such a strategy could prove dangerous to your portfolio's health. Developing a long-term perspective can be prudent yet amply rewarding. In this chapter, I provide guidance on how to choose companies suitable for long-term investing.

I recommend seven companies, which I identify as the Sweet Seven, that I think are appropriate for a buy-and-hold strategy for the next seven years. With these stocks, you can go on vacation and not worry about checking their prices—even if you should decide to go on a cruise around the world. Buy and hold doesn't mean buying stocks and forgetting about them altogether. No, it simply suggests that when you buy a stock, you should know how far you intend to run with it—it could be for a period longer than seven years, for instance—and what you expect in terms of returns.

Nobody should be permanently committed to a stock. There are instances when you do have to opt out, like when you realize you have made a grievous error in investing in a company. Leaving is a tough decision. If, for example, a company has significantly changed its business model and strategy, or if its CEO has been caught cooking the company's books, you might want to bail out fast. A lot of money has been lost by investors who won't walk away until they have broken even on their investments.

On the other hand, some cases present a more difficult situation. When, say, a pharmaceutical company gets bad news about one of its products, it may be a situation where the company can overcome the hurdles and prosper over the longer term because it has other new drugs in its pipeline. And indeed, the stock's drop might present a buying opportunity.

How should you go about pursuing a long-term strategy? As usual, you start with picking the right stocks. The wiser and easier way is to find really outstanding companies and stay with them through thick and thin even when the market gyrates in unpredictable fashion. That strategy has proven to be far more profitable to far more people than timing the market or fearlessly trading stocks. How do you find these outstanding companies? Certainly, a company's fundamentals have to be checked out. What is the company's image, including its leadership in the industry it's in? How "branded" or widely known are its products or services? What is the company's record on sales and earnings growth and return on capital, at least in the past five years? Check out the history of its stock price. Find out how smoothly or choppy it has performed over the past five years. The company's policies on shareholder enhancement and the integrity of its management team are important to scrutinize. All these require a lot of reading and research. Google and Yahoo.com are among the quick resources for this basic data.

Institutional investors mostly select the large-cap, well-known companies for their long-term portfolios. Of course, a large-cap stock can be as vulnerable to problems as the small-caps are. But size matters in choosing companies for the long run, because the bigger companies with large revenues and earnings bases, for instance, usually have a longer corporate history and are therefore more transparent. As such, they are able to provide answers to basic questions about prospects in the years ahead. In general, the background and performance record of the large-cap companies are much easier to track. In that sense, most of the blue chips and big-cap companies appear safer and less risky over the long haul. It figures that if there are problems or kinks along the way, these multiproduct giants could ride them out over the years. Because they have the financial resources to repair whatever could go wrong, these behemoth companies come out much-improved over the long run.

Going with the larger companies has worked well for many investors who have held on to such big stocks, like ExxonMobil, Apple, Procter & Gamble, and Colgate-Palmolive. Some of the large-caps, like ExxonMobil, do tremendously well because of their leadership in the industry—and because of the sharp rise in oil prices. Apple is another example of a giant winner because of its phenomenal new products and improving technology. Many others do just okay, with less than spectacular gains. But they do chalk up tremendous returns in certain years when their businesses are doing especially well. And those add up over the many years that they are in business and help register great returns.

Stocks for the short term obviously aim to grab instant rewards. The brief for long-term portfolios, however, is not just strong performance but the comfort of having a low beta or a less risky investment. Long-term players want to hold on to "safe" and dependable stocks that will not only endure but also post comparably pleasant gains and survive whatever stresses they bump into along the road.

Philip Fisher was wont to say, "I don't want a lot of good investments, I want a few outstanding ones." He was never inclined to sell a stock just because it provided good gains. An outstanding company, he asserted, can grow indefinitely. Some people might contest this type of thinking today. But Fisher believed that a stock that has risen in price substantially since its purchase only means that "everything is going just as it should." Indeed, a company that has demonstrated consistent rising growth rates over the years is worth buying for a long-term portfolio.

Except for the dyed-in-the-wool active trader, investing for the long term is the best market strategy to pursue. Traders do make money from the market's volatility, but they also take on colossal risks in the process. They are fired up by the speculative action the game provides. But they benefit the long-term investor—unwittingly, maybe. For example, if traders are shorting a stock that holds its own, that is a signal for the long-term investor to consider buying the stock.

Long-term investors usually have identified the stocks they want to own, but to get the current market temperament about them, there is nothing like the action that traders undertake to gauge investor sentiment. Of course, the market ultimately determines the true value of stocks over time. But when traders lampoon a stock and drive its price down, the patient long-term investor gets a chance to buy it at bargain levels—or at least at prices lower than he had bought them previously.

With enough patience, long-term investors decidedly benefit from the market's final verdict on stocks. Warren Buffett is the epitome of a patient, long-term investor who wisely gains from traders' activities. Like a totally focused lion, he waits on the sidelines until these traders have had their fun—or perhaps misery—going in and out of their targeted preys. After they have accomplished their goals, Buffett buys.

On the other hand, when furious activity by traders results in boosting a stock's price, unjustifiably or not, the long-term players can also benefit. That price hike will be tested. Investors with the patience and longer time perspective have the luxury of waiting it out to see if the stock holds this new price level after the traders have long since abandoned it. If it does, it is a signal that the stock has some mighty powerful fundamentals.

The market might cast its vote one way or the other over the short run, but a stock's real value surfaces over a longer period. In the end, a stock will stand or fall under the test of time. As I mentioned in an earlier chapter, long-term investors get an opportunity to profit from the market's short-term fluctuations by simply staying alert to opportunities mostly created by the traders. Many long-term investors have profited from such situations. Not all long-term investors are inclined to do so, however, but they could. When a stock goes up sharply and exceeds long-term targets in a portfolio, the investor has the option of slicing some profits without affecting the status as a core holding. That way, the investor will have the funds and the time to wait for the next bargain opportunity from the active traders frenzied activity. One of these stocks was U.S. Steel, whose shares stood at $12 each in 2001. By late 2002, U.S. Steel had jumped to $37 as demand for steel sprang up. The stock kept going and hit $93 in early 2007. Even before it hit the $90s, many long-term investors who had bought the stock at much lower prices bailed out as the stock reached their specific price targets.

To profit significantly from being a long-term holder, an investor needs to be conscientious in picking stocks. He must be able to endure price fluctuations and whatever else the market might throw its way during a long span of time. Necessarily, investors must make sure their chosen companies have the resources, tools, and skills to get to the victory lap at the designated time.

Generally, the best business to invest in, according to Buffett, is one that over time can employ large amounts of capital and get very high rates of return. Buffett has told shareholders of Berkshire Hathaway on several occasions that he is content with holding any stock indefinitely as long as he remains convinced that the potential return on equity capital is "satisfactory" and management remains honest and competent—and that the market hasn't unduly inflated the stock's valuation. That's a pretty tall order, but Berkshire Hathaway as an investment vehicle has produced such hefty returns. Berkshire Hathaway had about $46 billion in cash in its $61 billion portfolio at year-end 2006. Its stock, which trades at around $109,600 a share, has increased about 3,600 percent since 1978. Among Berkshire Hathaway's long-term holdings are *The Washington Post*, GEICO, and Coca-Cola.

Although I don't profess to be a Warren Buffett, I have chosen seven stocks that I believe will deliver outstanding returns over the next seven years. These are my choices based on my experience in the past quarter of a century in analyzing and writing about stocks, and from my interaction with hundreds of investment managers, analysts, and other investment professionals.

If I have to pick out one basic reason for my choices, it boils down to undervaluation. All these stocks are trading below their intrinsic value based on certain metrics, including their sales and earnings growth prospects. A stock may have attributes worth noting or faults to be concerned about. But if it is way undervalued relative to its peers, and if it's endowed with great prospects for growth, I would opt for the stock.

These Sweet Seven cover the areas of health care, energy, technology, and financial services. The importance of attending to the population's medical and health concerns is already upon us, but the dimension of this national problem will become even more acute as overwhelming diseases, such as cancer, become more widespread. The high cost of energy is another major concern. It affects every facet of life, and producers of oil and gas are the beneficiaries. Technology will also continue to affect everyone's life and change how people live, from wireless to smart phones, to newer and faster computers. And although the financial service companies have been hammered by the housing debacle and subprime mortgage crisis, they represent a wonderful opportunity for the long-term investor.

The following are the Sweet Seven companies that I expect will provide bountiful rewards for investors over the next seven years:

1. Apple (AAPL), the leading designer and maker of personal computers, the digital music player iPod, and the much vaunted iPhone

2. Boeing (BA), the world's second-largest commercial jet aircraft and military weapons manufacturer

3. CVS/Caremark Corp. (CVS), one of the largest U.S. drug store chain operators, with about 6,200 stores

4. Genentech (DNA), the largest biotechnology company

5. JPMorgan Chase & Co. (JPM), a leading global financial services company with assets of $1.3 trillion

6. Petróleo Brasileiro S.A. (PBR), Brazil's national oil and gas exploration, production, and refining company, trading on the Big Board with a market cap of $130 billion

7. Pfizer (PFE), the world's largest pharmaceutical company

The Innovative Apple

What qualifies Apple to be a seven-year core portfolio holding? The answer: innovation, innovation, innovation. You may add to that: practical and sleek products, futuristic business strategies, and a management team led by visionary Steve Jobs. This particular CEO has demonstrated skilled staying power and prowess in an industry where even great technological advances can be fleeting and obsolescent in a snap. He has proven time and again that he is a creative manager who can keep Apple at the top of its game. Of course, critics predict his downfall sooner or later. However, Jobs' wizardry in sprinting a step or two ahead of the competition will be a big challenge for them. He has built a company of the future with novel, futuristic products.

What's next from the imaginative management team at Apple? After the novel Macintosh PCs and the cleverly designed iPod digital media player, followed by its recent marvel, the sleek multifunctional iPhone, it is hard to imagine what will come next from Apple's production table. The incomparable iPhone, a wireless phone that combines the features of the iPod with an Internet communications system, has become a sensation. Analysts expected Apple to sell 2.2 million iPhones by the end of 2007. Apple has come out with new versions of the iPod—a larger-screen iPod nano, a higher capacity iPod classic, and a full-screen iPod with Internet access. The buzz is that Apple is on its way to way to producing a next-generation iPhone that will operate super fast and respond to the many demands of iPhone users.

With such a line of impressive products, Apple is no longer just a computer company, although it is still selling a lot of its fancy mighty Mac machines. Sales have been growing at three times the growth of the industry. Apple rolled out an upgraded operating system in late 2007 that would include software to enable users to run Windows applications.

Apple's share of the $200 billion PC market is relatively small, estimated by analysts at about 5 percent. But the iPod dominates the fast-growing MP3 player market. Research firm IDC estimates MP3 industry sales at $21 billion in 2005, and it figures that they grew by about 30 percent in 2006. The growing popularity of the iPod, which now accounts for some 40 percent of Apple's total revenues, has helped boost the sales of Mac computers.

Apple shares have also been a phenomenal marvel to watch. It was not too long ago—in mid-2001, when Apple's stock traded as low as $7.50 a share. And then the iPod was born the following year. In 2003, Apple launched the iTunes digital download service for the iPod. iTunes has about 85 percent share of the legal download music market, according to Apple. In 2005, television video content was added to iPod. The stock started moving in 2004, from $10 a share, reaching $38 at year-end. Since then, the stock has built its own high-way in the sky. On December 28, 2007, the stock skyrocketed to $199.83.

Looking at its price-earnings (p/e) multiple of 42, based on esti-mated 2008 earnings of $4.80 a share, might discourage investors who focus on or prefer lower p/es, but taken along with its p/e to growth (PEG) ratio of 1.3 times, it is comparable to the PEG ratio of the S&P technology sector. The stock continues to be attractive despite its straight-up ascent because it deserves a premium valuation over its peers as the company's brand has become a worldwide name, with vast opportunities for further growth. W. Smith of S&P noted in a report on the company that Apple continues to benefit from its strat-egy of providing simple but superior products. The iPhone, he adds, will be notably accretive to earnings, reflecting "solid sales and considerable associated customer traffic." A healthy balance sheet enhances Apple's financials, consisting of $14.5 billion in net cash and investments as of September 2007, equivalent to $17.71 a share. There is a possibility, Smith figures, that Apple may repurchase shares at some point because of its significant cash hoard.

In sum, Apple's focus on a strategy of producing superior and sophisticated products is pushing the company ahead of its rivals. Apple's increasing market share in desktop and notebook computers, and leadership in the digital music player business with iPod—and now enhanced by the launching of the iPhone system—assure the company of increased bright prospects ahead. These gains plus Steve Jobs's vision for Apple to stay a superior company well into the future should give long-term investors confidence that Apple is not only here to stay, but also should lead in the fields it chooses to be in. It has become so attractive that it wouldn't be a surprise if, within a year, Apple becomes buyout prey to a larger company, like Google or Microsoft.

Boeing—The High-Flying Super Machine

Boeing (BA) is a formidable company that deserves a place in any long-term core portfolio. It is an all-around aerospace company. A leading maker of commercial jet aircraft, it also manufactures jet fighters, such as the F-15 and F/A-18, as well as the V-22 helicopter and the C-17 cargo carrier. But that's not all. The world's second largest commercial airplane maker also develops and builds space stations.

Industry analysts agree that Boeing's sales and earnings will climb rapidly in the coming years, as evidenced by the company's order backlog of $262 billion, which is more than four times its estimated

2007 revenues of $65 million. With that kind of a backlog and strong order flow, Boeing should produce robust earnings and sustained cash flow growth for many years to come. Orders for its commercial airplanes reached 1,047 in November of 2007, a third consecutive annual record. Boeing has been managing its R&D costs quite well. Despite the big cost behind the making of the company's newest wide body 787 Dreamliner aircraft—about $1 billion—margins continue to widen fast, bolstered mainly by production efficiency fueled by higher sales volume. Demand for the Dreamliner, scheduled to start flying in late 2008, has been overwhelming. Boeing has won orders from 47 clients for more than 600 Dreamliners, worth $114 billion in sales— well beyond the 500 that analysts expected. Boeing wants to make sure that its many suppliers will be in a position to meet the company's increasing needs should it find it necessary to boost production levels because of rising demand. Orders had been so strong in recent years that it was a pleasant surprise to Boeing that order flow continued to be robust in 2007.

On the company's military production, orders for its military systems have continued to swell, as well. Analysts predict that whoever wins the U.S. presidential elections in 2008 will not alter the demand for Boeing's military aircraft and technology, which include the E-3 AWACS and E-6 submarine communicator system.

Shares of Boeing have been on an upward course since 2003, when it was selling at $24 a share. It flew to an all-time high of $107 by July 2007. As of December 31, 2007, the stock had eased to $87.46, trading at just 16 times analysts' 2008 consensus earnings estimate of $6 a share—below its peer average of 17.2. Profit projections are also in an upward trend: for 2009, $7.50 on revenues of $80.8 billion, and for 2010, $8.60 a share on $85.6 billion, up from an estimated $5 in 2007 on $66.2 billion, and 2006's $3.62 on $61.5 billion.

Boeing is in the pink of financial health, repurchasing shares and boosting its dividend payments. There aren't many high-flying super giants in their prime of success that aren't saddled with major financial problems. Boeing, to be sure, is an appropriate core holding in any long-term portfolio.

CVS Caremark Corp: The Number-One Value Drug Store Chain

Some astounding facts about CVS Caremark: (1) The largest U.S. pharmaceutical chain fills more than one billion—yes, one billion— prescriptions a year, which account for 70 percent of sales. (2) Its pharmacy benefit management business, which provides drug benefit services to health plan sponsors and their participants, covers more than 30 million lives, and it is estimated to have produced sales of $75.8 billion in 2007. (3) Over an eight-year period, CVS's total sales grew annually at an impressive compounded rate of 24 percent a year. (4) Wall Street loves CVS. As of December 31, 2007, none of the 21 major analysts who track the stock had a sell recommendation—not a common occurrence. Sixteen of the analysts advised clients to buy the stock, and four rated it a hold or neutral. (5) The stock was one of the few that weathered both the Chinese stock market decline in February 2007 and the crash in the summer and autumn of that same year that was caused by the subprime-mortgage crisis. (6) Shares of CVS have for years performed extremely well: They climbed from a low of $11 a share in 2001 to a high of $39 on May 25, 2007. On November 13, 2007, at the height of the subprime storm, CVS was aloft at a 52-week high of $42.25.

CVS nearly doubled its sales when it acquired CaremarkRx for about $26.5 billion in March 2007. The merger combined two of the largest pharmacy benefit managers in the U.S. The year before the merger, CVS produced total sales in 2006 of $43.8 billion. For 2008, analysts project sales of $89.5 billion, and for 2009, $96 billion. Continued positive sales growth and upbeat margin trends are in the cards, mainly due to acquisitions that have brought in a pipeline of new products.

CVS, which stands for Consumer Value Store, is a relatively young company. It started as a health and beauty aids chain in 1963 and grew into 17 stores by 1964. It was in 1967 that CVS started its first pharmacy. In 1969, a company called Melville acquired CVS and expanded its operations. Melville acquired Revco, a drug-store chain, and Arbor Drug. In 1995, Melville restructured itself, and a year later it adopted the name CVS. As of December 31, 2007, it had 6,200 locations in 43 states—and it's growing every year.

In spite of its steady ascent, CVS's stock is trading at a modest valuation, with a p/e ratio of 17 times estimated 2008 earnings of $2.31 a share for the following year. That p/e multiple is below its ten-year average p/e of 22.4—and also below that of its peers. With analysts forecasting continued growth in sales and earnings in the years ahead, the stock will likely continue to drive up, consistent with its advance since 1997, when it traded at $9 a share. Given that kind of energetic history, the stock could hit at least $100 in seven years. With its prospects for increased growth, CVS Caremark is a worthy core holding for a long-term portfolio.

Genentech: The Biotech Behemoth

Genentech easily stands out as the leader in the fast-growing universe of biotechnology, clearly focused on developing novel biotherapeutics against cancer and autoimmune disorders. It is an easy selection for a long-term portfolio. Although it is number one in cancer drugs, there is worry that its blockbuster drug, Avastin, might be headed for a sales slowdown. Because Avastin accounts for 23 percent of Genentech's total product sales, the concern is legitimate. Part of the worry stems from a study that concludes that Avastin works marginally better when used in half the standard dosage. So Wall Street was fast to anticipate that physicians would henceforth prescribe lower doses, thus reducing Avastin sales. The drug was approved in 2004, for first-time treatment of metastatic colorectal cancer. Switzerland's Roche Holdings owns a controlling 55.8 percent stake in Genentech, and it holds the marketing rights on Avastin outside the U.S.

Word of the study put a damper on Genentech's stock, tumbling from $89 a share in mid-January 2007 to $74 by August 31, 2007. Avastin's sales in 2006 totaled $1.75 billion, but analysts were disappointed that sales in 2007's second quarter were just about even with the previous quarter's. Never mind that management expects Avastin sales to jump because of its approval for treatment of lung cancer. Avastin is also expected to be approved in mid-2008 for the treatment of breast cancer. That surely bodes well for future sales. Investors have made a bundle on Genentech's stock, which started moving upward in 2002 from a low of $12.50. By 2005, the stock had rocketed to $100.20. However, it started to cool down, and by the summer of 2007, the stock had dropped to $74. That was quite a jaw-dropping fall because, earlier in the year, the stock had climbed to $89 due to a meteoric jump in sales and earnings. Sales had climbed from $4.6 billion in 2004 to $9.2 billion in 2006; earnings advanced from 73 cents a share in 2004 to $1.97 in 2006. On December 31, 2007, the stock closed at $67.07 a share.

Despite some analysts' downcast view of Genentech, the company's sales and earnings should grow 25 percent to 30 percent annually over the next five years. In 2008, the company is expected to build up sales to nearly $12.9 billion, with earnings rising to $3.12 a share. In 2009, sales are estimated to leap to some $14.4 billion on earnings of $3.87 a share.

There is much to be optimistic about Genentech's product pipeline. Genentech has an impressive line of existing life-saving drugs, as well as an equally dazzling array of medicines in the making.

Management told analysts in 2007 that it started 13 compounds into new drugs in 18 months. The goal is to have 30 drugs in development by 2010. Genentech's lineup of existing drugs include Rituxan for non-Hodgkins lymphoma, which accounted for 24 percent of sales in 2006; Herceptin for breast cancer, 14 percent of sales; Xolair for asthma, 5 percent; and Tarceva for lung cancer, 4 percent. Some of the new areas that Genentech hopes to conquer are autoimmune diseases, such as multiple sclerosis, currently a $5 billion market, and rheumatoid arthritis, a $10 billion market that is growing at about 30 percent a year.

The low expectations for Genentech make the stock a perfect bullish call for the next seven years. Some analysts continue to expect upbeat earnings at least over the next five years. Value Line, for one, says in a mid-2007 report that Genentech's R&D pipeline continues to be impressive and should support above-average profit growth over the next three to five years. Ultimately, it is quite likely that the company will embark on more acquisitions to add to its already substantial pipeline of existing and future drugs. Rumors are starting to catch in that regard, and with Wall Street's unchanging mentality that acquisitions are a reason to bail out of an acquiring company's stock, more opportunities may lie ahead to buy shares of Genentech at a greater bargain. But at this point, Genentech is already a heck of a bargain, especially if you keep the stock as a long-term holding.

JPMorgan Chase & Co.: Up on Wall Street and Main Street

JPMorgan Chase is a bank for all seasons. A well-diversified global financial services company, this storied institution has many avenues of further growth around the world, in practically all sectors of business and finance. Yet it is not an unwieldy enterprise. Its six major businesses operate in an orderly fashion—especially since James

"Jamie" Dimon took over the helm as chief executive in 2005—aimed at pursuing global growth. The ultimate goal is to be the top U.S. financial institution, eclipsing current number one, Citigroup.

This is Dimon's inexorable ambition—to trounce Citigroup and become king of the domain. One overwhelming reason is that Dimon was mentored and nurtured by the previous banking king, Sandy Weill, who spearheaded Citigroup's ascent to fortune and fame. Citigroup topped the banking world under Weill. Dimon started as an assistant to Weill many years ago. Before long, he ascended to the right of King Weill, attaining the much sought-after status of heir to the throne. It almost happened but didn't. Dimon had problems with Weill's daughter, who was also starting to gain power at Citigroup. In the end, Dimon left the comfort of being Weill's prospective heir and moved on. And moved he did.

When he joined JPMorgan in 2004 through the merger of Bank One, of which he was the CEO, and JPMorgan to form JPMorgan Chase & Co., there was little doubt that he would ascend to the top spot of the combined institutions. And well he did. But the rest is not yet history. Dimon is still well on his way to driving JPMorgan up the mountain of ultimate fortune, fame, and power. So my forecast is that, through the economy's ups and down and market volatility, JPMorgan Chase's work has been cut out for it: Onward and forward.

These are not the only reasons why I pick JPMorgan for a spot in the seven-stocks-for-seven-years portfolio. For starters, the company is superbly managed, a hard task given its financial conglomerate structure. Dimon has it so structured that it has amassed the financial strength and resources to capture market share during times of crisis, as what happened in the summer and autumn of 2007 with the onset of the subprime mortgage problem. In other words, JPMorgan has the financial capacity to benefit from any market disruption, such as the ability to act quickly as a financial mediator given its financial capital and balance-sheet strength. Mike Mayo, banking analyst at

Deutsche Bank, estimates that U.S. fixed income and mortgages comprise 20 percent of the company's business, but only one-fifth of that involves subprime and leveraged lending. So Mayo lowered his earnings estimates for 2008 by just five cents a share, to $3.53 a share. In 2006, JPMorgan earned $4.03 a share and an estimated $4.68 in 2007.

JPMorgan operates in more than 50 countries, with total assets of $1.45 trillion—yes, trillion. Analysts estimate those assets will leap to $15.5 trillion by the end of 2007, and to $16.5 trillion in 2008. Its six lines of business are investment banking, retail financial services, commercial banking, card services, treasury and securities services, and asset management.

In the investment banking world, JPMorgan's name is rock solid: Its clients consist of the top corporations, financial institutions, governments, and institutional investors worldwide. Its retail financing unit covers anything your home or family might need, from consumer and small-business banking to auto and education loans. JPMorgan Chase banks have mushroomed all over the country, to more than 3,000 bank branches in the U.S., with close to 9,000 ATMs. These don't include the 339 branches it acquired from Bank of New York in 2006. Its credit card business is also huge, with 154 cards in circulation and $153 billion in managed loans as of the end of 2006. JPMorgan is the second-largest issuer of MasterCard and Visa credit cards. In treasury and securities, the amount that JPMorgan oversees is staggering: $13.9 trillion at year-end 2006—up 30 percent from 2005's total. It is estimated that the same amount of increase will be realized in the next several years. Its asset under management, $1 trillion, is still a gigantic amount.

In sum, JPMorgan "covers the water front," from Wall Street to Main Street. Its stock has not been a stunner in performance, which was shot down (but not as much as the other financial institutions) when the market was scorched during the subprime mortgage crisis in the summer of 2007. But, for a financial institution, JPMorgan's stock has not done so poorly. It traded as low as $15 a share in 2002 but, by May 2007, the stock hit a high of $53. However, the stock backed down to $43.65 by December 31, 2007, in part because of the subprime mortgage mess. Frank Braden of S&P expects the stock to climb to $58 in 2008, based on his earnings forecast for the year of $4.90. Resilient credit quality trends at the retail and commercial banking, along with healthy capital markets activity, will position the company to show solid earnings growth, according to Braden. The poor results from mortgage banking, auto financing, and the leveraged loan business, however, could be a near-term drag.

Over the longer term, JPMorgan's stock is bound to be a triple hit, maybe more, if the growth trajectory of Dimon's team is sustained. Despite its storied, respected name, JPMorgan's earnings power continues to be underestimated by Wall Street. Yet, with its solid growth prospects, diverse geographic reach, multiple products, and large customer base worldwide, JPMorgan has the financial muscle, energy, and will not only to confront challenges ahead but also to achieve its mighty and lofty growth goals.

Petróleo Brasileiro S.A.: An All-Around Energy Play

If you want a stock that represents practically everything in an energy stock, Petróleo Brasileiro (commonly referred to as Petrobras) is your best bet. The fourteenth largest oil company in the world, Petrobras is controlled by Brazil's national government but trades on the New York Stock Exchange through its American Depositary Receipts, or ADRs. One ADR represents one common share of Petrobras. Some 16 percent of its shares are publicly traded on both the Big Board and Brazil's stock exchange.

Look at Petrobras's fundamentals: Its growth rate, profitability, returns, assets efficiency, and financial health are strong when compared to its peers in emerging markets, as well as relative to the U.S. and European major oil companies. Christian Audi, an analyst at Spain's Santander Investment Securities, who is a big believer in the company, expects Petrobras's operating momentum in 2008 to strengthen. Looking beyond 2008, Petrobras's fundamentals continue to compare favorably with its main oil peers in the emerging markets—particularly China and Russia—as well as with the super majors in North America and Europe, says Audi.

Petrobras combines elements that many global oil companies lack and which energy investors look for: new discoveries, strong reserve position, continued production growth potential, and a refinery infrastructure that's capable of generating solid refining margins. Speaking of discoveries, on September 5, 2007, Petrobras announced that it found light oil in a well 170 miles off Brazil's coast in Santos Basin. Analysts project that it might produce 2,900 barrels of oil and 57,000 cubic meters of natural gas a day. Petrobras owns a 45 percent stake in the block, BG Group has 30 percent, and Spanish-Argentine firm Repsol holds 25 percent. The company is optimistic about finding future oil in the area because of the latest discovery's proximity to Petrobras's Tupi oil field, where the company discovered light oil in October 2006. In this Tupi field, Petrobras owns 65 percent, with BG holding 25 percent, and Petróleos de Portugal 10 percent.

Petrobras plans to start producing oil and natural gas from its Tupi field by the end of 2010. The company estimates oil production from the Tupi field at 100,000 barrels a day. Petrobras figures that Tupi is the second largest oil field found in the world in the last 20 years and holds as much as 8 billion barrels of oil and natural gas equivalent.

Another significance of the latest find is that it is located near the Mexilho field where Petrobras and BG plan to start producing some nine million cubic meters a day of natural gas in 2009.

Not surprisingly, there is a lot of excitement about the latest discovery and its ramifications. The oil find may well lead to increased production of light oil. So far, most of Petrobras's oil production is from heavy oil, which is priced at a discount to lighter crude oil. Obviously, lighter crude would boost profits for Petrobras. In addition, Petrobras plans to drill the first natural gas exploration well in the Caribbean Sea off the coast of Columbia in partnership with Exxon-Mobil and Ecopetrol SA. They might find as much as 10 trillion cubic feet, according to Armando Zamora, director general of Columbia's National Hydrocarbon Agency, in a speech before the Offshore Europe Conference in Aberdeen, Scotland in 2007.

Here is the extent of Petrobras's operations: It is active in all segments of the oil business. In 2006, its oil and exploration accounted for 81 percent of operating earnings and 29 percent of revenues; refining operations brought in 20 percent of earnings and 47 percent of sales; the distribution unit, including nearly 6,000 retail service stations, accounted for 2 percent of earnings and 15 percent of sales; its natural gas activities, which involve the sale and transportation of natural gas produced or imported into Brazil—including commercialization of domestic electric—produced 4 percent of profits and 4 percent of sales; and its international business, including oil and gas drilling in West Africa, the Gulf of Mexico in the U.S., and South America, pulled in 1 percent and 5 percent. In all of these, Petrobras operates oil tankers, distribution pipelines, and marine terminals. Petrobras also operates thermal power plants, fertilizer and petrochemical facilities.

How much oil does Petrobras, which operates in 27 countries, produce? According to its own forecasts, 2007 production totaled an average of 1.858 million barrels of oil a day from its domestic fields, and 2.050 million barrels a day in 2008. By 2012, Petrobras expects oil and gas production in Brazil alone of 3.058 million barrels of oil equivalents a day, and by 2015 it expects to produce about 3.455 million barrels a day. In 2006, production totaled 2.055 million barrels a day. Combined with overseas oil production, total output would amount to 3,494 million barrels a day in 2012 and 4,153 million in 2015.

Ethanol plays a part in the equation. Petrobras predicts that ethanol and natural gas will comprise more than half of the fuel used by Brazilian automobiles in 2008. Gasoline as a motor fuel will drop to 44 percent of the Brazilian market from 60 percent. Brazil is the world's second largest ethanol producer after the U.S. The U.S. produces ethanol mainly from corn, while Brazil, the world's largest sugar cane producer, uses sugar cane. Petrobras isn't yet producing ethanol, but it is highly active in the ethanol business because its pipelines and oil tankers are used by the government in transporting the product. Among the importers of Brazil's ethanol are the U.S., Japan, and Korea. Ethanol production is expected to jump to 4.75 billion liters in 2012, up from 500 million liters in 2008. It is likely that Petrobras will go into the production of ethanol.

Santander Investment Securities forecasts that Petrobas will earn $13 billion in 2008 on sales of $77.8 billion, and $14.1 billion in 2009 on sales of $79.6 billion, up from an estimated $12.3 billion in 2007 on sales of $75.6 billion.

Some of the major U.S. institutional investors are large stakeholders in Petrobras, including Capital Research Management, which owns 3.5 percent; Fidelity Management, with 2.6 percent; and Marsico Capital, with 1.5 percent. The stock bucked the tide during the market's plunge in the summer of 2007 and has continued to rise—from $36 in September 2006 to $115.24 on December 31, 2007. Despite the stock's stunning rise, Petrobras trades with a p/e of 21, considered by analysts to be modest considering the company's extraordinarily strong growth prospects. Over the next seven years, some investors expect the stock to at least quadruple. Summing up Petrobras's attraction as a long-term holding, the stock is an energy play as well as a bet on Brazil's fast economic growth as an emerging market.

Pfizer, Inc.: The King of Big Pharma

Being number one in any endeavor is almost a punishment in the sense that massive pressure is constantly building up on the leader to keep the throne. But there is no substitute for being number one. Pfizer, the world's largest pharmaceutical company, is in that enviable, yet stressful position. It is an unending battle to stay on top, so it isn't surprising that Pfizer is redoubling efforts to make sure it keeps up with its growth targets to stay ahead of its peers.

In 2007, doubts mounted to such a level that Wall Street started to embrace doubts that the premier drugmaker might, indeed, disappoint analysts' lofty expectations. Most analysts turned cold on Pfizer—of the 28 major analysts who track Pfizer, 18 rated the stock a hold or neutral, 2 recommended sell, and 8 advised investors to buy. Nonetheless, investors would be well advised to remember that Pfizer did not get to the top by being a lazy benchwarmer.

In the $670 billion global pharmaceutical industry, Pfizer is a giant that generated sales of $48.3 billion in 2006. Its fast growth in the past ten years was achieved mainly through some wise large acquisitions. It acquired Warner Lambert Co. in 2000 and Pharmacia in 2003. Pfizer is apt to embark again on significant acquisitions to ignite the torch for renewed growth and fire up its stock once again. Pfizer also does a lot of partnership deals with other companies, mainly biotechs, to develop new drugs. Some 25 percent of Pfizer's discoveries and drug development work comes from such partnerships. New products being developed include Maraviroc, an inhibitor for the treatment of HIV/AIDS; Sutent, or sunitinib malate, a multikinase inhibitor that has been approved for the treatment of advanced renal cell carcinoma and gastrointestinal tumors; and Chantix for smoking cessation. In October 2007, Pfizer pulled one of its products from the market, Exubera, an inhaled insulin, after doctors expressed concern about its long-term safety. Pfizer took a $2.8

billion writeoff on Exubera, a medication that provided diabetes patients an alternative to injected insulin. Pfizer had predicted that Exubera would produce sales of $2 billion a year.

In the case of Maraviroc, an FDA panel voted unanimously to recommend it for approval, and Pfizer got an approvable letter in June 2007. Pfizer is working with the FDA to finalize product labeling. On Sutent, Pfizer initiated in September 2007 a global Phase III clinical trial to evaluate its efficacy and safety in treating patients with advanced non-small cell lung cancer. Lung cancer is the leading cause of cancer in men and women around the world. Some 60 percent of lung cancer patients are diagnosed late with stage IIB-IV advanced disease, and most of them have evidence of distant metastasis at the time of the diagnosis, according to Pfizer studies. So Maraviroc will be a vital product for Pfizer.

Pfizer's organic growth will be rekindled by its robust pipeline of new drugs in the works. In 2006, it spent $7.6 billion, or 15 percent of total revenues, on research and development. Its pipeline includes about 184 novel compounds or potential new molecular entities, as well as product-enhancement projects. Pfizer's drug pipeline covers treatments for obesity, arthritis, heart disease, and cancer.

That, however, hasn't cheered analysts, most of whom have gotten tired of waiting for some fire from Pfizer. They expected revenues to drop about three percent from 2007 through 2009. Nonetheless, consensus earnings expectations are upbeat: They are expected to increase from 2006's $2.06 a share to $2.22 in 2007, $2.31 in 2008, and $2.50 in 2009. However, analysts believe it is "show-me" time for Pfizer for them to turn bullish again.

I am convinced that Pfizer will regain ascendancy and that signs of a forceful recovery will surface for it to stay on top. Here is the background of what's happening. With Pfizer's revenue growth expected to remain under downward pressure in the short term, mainly because of the scheduled expiration of patents of its major growth drivers, such as Lipitor and Norvasc, the company's shares have languished. Pfizer's patent on Lipitor, the world's largest selling cholesterol-lowering agent—and the biggest in any drug category in 2006 (it produced sales of nearly $13 billion)—expires in 2011. During a 12-month period ended November 21, 2007, the stock meandered between $22 and $28 a share. In its glory days not too long ago, in 1999, the stock traded as high as $50, adjusted for a three-for-one split that year.

Clearly, Pfizer needs to replace the $13 billion in revenue that might be lost when Lipitor goes off patent in 2011. A couple of generics have already cut into Lipitor sales. But Pfizer hasn't been idle about this. It is trying to boost sales from its existing cache of products and cutting costs and restructuring its operations to boost innovation, productivity, and accountability.

Some 38 drugs are now in Phase II clinical trials, and five are in Phase III. Pfizer's drug pipeline is its largest ever.

For investors who are patiently waiting for things to happen to rejuvenate Pfizer's valuation, the company's large payout, equal to a dividend yield of 4.5 percent, is a worthwhile reward for keeping cool. Meanwhile, the company's robust cash position gives the company the flexibility to license new compounds and jump on any opportunity to partner with companies for new drugs. Pfizer, as I have said, will embark on more acquisitions, but the immediate ones would likely be midsize purchases to produce new drugs without interrupting its efforts in streamlining its current restructuring. And expect some share buybacks along the way.

Pfizer has dropped to such bargain-basement levels ($22 a share on December, 31 2007), that combined with the Street's ho-hum attitude toward the stock, King Pfizer is a great buy for the next seven years. Positive news about an acquisition or product will fire up the stock and give it the momentum to fly. Or, a not uncommon event might develop:

An activist investor like Carl Icahn might enter the picture and jolt management into action. That is not an impossible scenario. As I have said before, investors should expect the unexpected.

There you have it: the Sweet Seven for the next seven years. They are in the sweet spot of investing, to have and to hold for a prosperous future.

The charts of the Seven Stocks for the Next Seven Years on the following pages show the performance of each stock over a 12-month period, from January 3, 2007 to December 31, 2007.

AAPL Equity

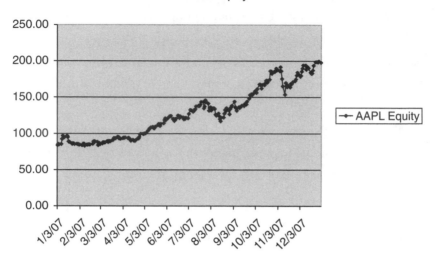

BA Equity

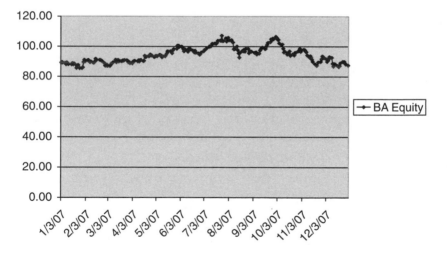

CVS Equity

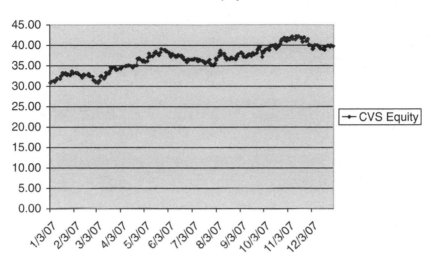

DNA Equity

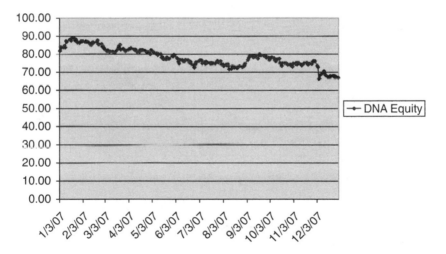

JPM Equity

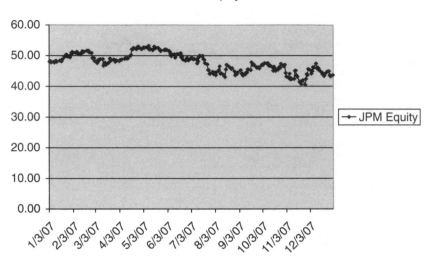

PBR Equity

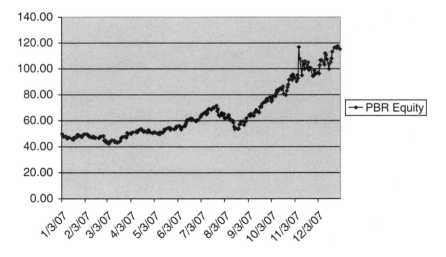

PFE Equity

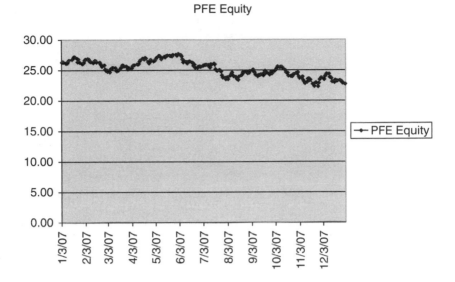

EPILOGUE

My hope is that, after reading this book, you, as an investor, will have changed your mind-set about stock investing. You need not worry about whether the market will sink or soar. Whatever direction the market takes, you should have the will and readiness to act and harvest the opportunities it presents. Investors are in the market to grab the opportunity to buy at bargain prices or to sell at profitable levels. If you prepare for eventualities that could torpedo the market—such as the subprime mortgage mess—as the first chapter of this book advocates (Buy Panic), you will be a winner rather than a worrier. As I have emphasized repeatedly in this book, it is difficult to think of buying stocks when the market is crashing. It is just as difficult to sell stocks when the market is soaring. But your new mind-set should dictate that these are the opportunities to make money.

The events in 2007 and January 2008 resulted in a major market meltdown as the impact of the subprime mortgage maelstrom and the credit crunch reverberated across America and in many parts of the globe. After rocketing to an all-time record high on October 7, 2007, at 14,164.53, the Dow Jones industrial average tumbled the next month, on November 23, 2007, by 195.91 points, to 12,980.88. The decline didn't stop there. It spilled over to the new year of 2008. On January 11, 2008, the Dow dropped 193.88 points, to 12,606.30.

If anything, the events of the past year and early 2008 made my book more germane—even more germane, in fact, than when I started writing it on January 31, 2007, when the Dow stood at

12,647.21. The market at that time was selling at a bargain, but now the market has much more stocks to offer that are selling at truly super fire-sale prices.

My advice in Chapter 1, Commandment One, on Buy Panic is even more suitable and appropriate now in the market's current condition. It suggests that in times of panic, investors should be prepared to jump on opportunities and buy those bushwhacked stocks. Citigroup, for one, was a big bargain at $35 a share before the subprime mess got really messy. The stock hit a low of 27 on January 7, 2008. That was an even bigger steal for investors.

Major financial institutions, including Citigroup, Bank of America, Bear Stearns, Wachovia, Merrill Lynch, and Morgan Stanley, owned up to losses of many billions of dollars from write-downs of securities that were exposed to the troubled subprime mortgage loans.

As dark as the skies appeared over the financial and housing sectors, the situation created an oversupply of great bargains in other sectors, such as technology and health care, which also became hammered as the subprime contagion spread. Again, I felt that investors were swayed by the panicky crowd and joined the massive selling that took place. We have seen this show before, with the same painful results, culminating, however, in the market's strong rebound thereafter.

So many books have been written about the stock market and stock investing, so what could I add? Plenty, in my humble opinion. Many of those books—thoughtful, intelligent, and informative as they are—do not alter the hapless and helpless ways individual investors respond to the market when it gets shaken up by events. The principal goal of my book is just that: Change individual investors' mind-set about stock investing to better prepare them to seize opportunities in harvesting bonanzas from stocks.

The stock market is the ultimate capitalist's tool, to borrow a line from *Forbes'* slogan. The market is the only place on the planet where you can become a millionaire overnight. Of course, you could also lose as much, instantly, in a minute of indiscretion or sloppy judgment. The plain truth is that the odds are very much against the non-professional investor from the outset.

Individuals like you are handicapped by two things. The first is that you're playing against the seasoned professionals, mainly the institutional investors, armed with all the resources to trump you. The second element that hampers you is your own conflicting emotions of fear, greed, and every other human foible and emotion clashing within your being.

To know that these two elements are enemies to conquer is the first step to winning.

How do you bet against the pros in a market notorious for its unpredictable sways when you are, at the same time, pulled and pushed every which way by your conflicting emotions? To add to this problem, the institutional investors, apart from being armed with all the technology and computer science that the modern digital world can provide, have the money to overwhelm the market. The stock market plays no favorites and is investor-neutral. Don't expect any help from it. The market does what it will whenever it wants.

One reason it is difficult for individual investors to fathom the market and win is because it is composed of investors like you and the institutional money managers. The stock market is the conglomeration of investors of every stripe and persuasion, from every corner of the world. And globalization has made the situation even more difficult for the individual investor. The competition is now guaranteed to be global in force and resources.

As global as the equity market is, the big institutional investors control and dominate it. Despite the rules and regulations in the U.S. markets to safeguard investors' interests and ensure fairness, the playing field is far from even.

In Las Vegas, the "house" seldom loses. On Wall Street, the big institutions are the equivalent of the "house." They control the market, although some of them manage to lose money, but not too often and not without recourse. When the market tumbled during the 2007 credit crisis, few investors were spared from financial pain. But the institutional investors were better prepared than the individual investors. They initiated the selling and did not suffer as much as the individuals, who followed their selling. Often, the institutions are able to lock in their profits by selling early when the market is riding high instead of selling after it has tanked. Most of the initial selling is initiated by the quants and daily traders, who invariably establish a bearish bent to the market. Hopefully, the individual investors who followed the selling by institutions were getting rid of stocks that yielded profits rather than losses.

The institutions dominate about 75 percent to 80 percent of the market's liquidity—the daily buying and selling of stocks. They have diverse methods or models to make the most money. But their power is evident when they act in unison, which usually ends up trampling the small, individual investors.

With the situation so tilted in favor of the market's big leaguers, how can individual investors win or even survive in the stock market? As I mentioned earlier, you should adopt a particularly out-of-the-mainstream mind-set. The institutions win in large measure because they know the mentality of the market's small players, known as the "retail" investors, meaning you, the individual investor, whose accounts in the brokerage houses are labeled retail accounts. Many individual investors are smarter and savvier than the pros, but they are at a disadvantage because they don't have as much clout as the institutions.

The institutions expect the retail crowd to follow in their footsteps—by about a mile behind them. The institutions buy far ahead of the crowd and sell way ahead of them. By the time the individual investors get wind of what stocks the big players are buying, the institutional players are already downloading or bailing out of those same stocks, leaving the retail accounts holding the bag.

That leaves the individual investors behind the eight ball. If they are nimble enough or play the trading game, they might garner some profits. But they often give up most of whatever gains they make for a lot of reasons outside their control, such as not being quick enough to take profits, or the market going south sooner than expected. In the end, playing the trading game is a losing proposition, as many of the so-called **day traders** in the 1980s found out soon enough. Flipping stocks, or buying shares today and selling them the next minute, hour, or day, is extremely risky. There is no substitute for long-term investing.

For the most part, individual investors become victims of the market's tumultuous ways because of what I call the **Panic Doctrine**. Panic governs the market and is the paramount producer of market crashes or rallies. As the first chapter, "Buy Panic," advocates, investors should prepare for periods when the market is gripped by panic. I cannot overemphasize this maxim. That is the only way the investor can approach the market with confidence and equanimity.

Otherwise, the market's unpredictable twists and turns will always leave the investor hanging, holding the proverbial empty bag. Why does this happen year in and year out? Human nature usually plays up to what is popular, what is in fashion. The result is, when panic seizes the market, the individual investor buys when everybody else is buying, and sells when the crowd is selling. That is the essence of **herd mentality**—following the crowd—and it's a sure pathway to the loser's corner.

What is required is the discipline, determination, and guts to not only go against the tide but also to steadfastly execute what must be done. If it requires buying shares of Apple when they are plunging five percent or more—and you know that the problem causing the drop has little do with the company's fundamentals—you should determinedly buy, period. When most investors are buying shares of a company because the industry it is in is hot, such as the solar industry, and the stock is soaring as a result, you should sell or short the stock—

if you know or have evidence that the fundamentals of the company will sour if not go bust in a year or so. That is the kind of discipline you need to win decisively. It is neither arrogance nor stubbornness. It is discipline based on common sense and intelligence.

The unprecedented events that started in 2007 demonstrated how Wall Street's Big Shots and the elitist Masters of the Universe, including the major investment bankers and managers and market mavens, could and did make gigantic mistakes in judgment and execution. It is a jolting wake-up call for those who have the most expensive alarm clocks and alert devices.

The question that is frequently asked when people walk by the marinas filled with luxurious yachts that mostly belong to stockbrokers is, "Where are the yachts of their customers/investors?" Well, you can bet that today, there are much fewer yachts on the marinas that belong to stockbrokers.

How the subprime troubles will be resolved and how long the housing recession will last are far from clear. And how the stock market will behave and perform from here on is anybody's guess. Sure, the confusion and consternation that the subprime and credit-crunch problems unleashed caused the market to tumble and hurt investors. But such situations produce ample bargain opportunities, and my book's Seven Commandments of Stock Investing would definitely be a godsend to investors caught in that predicament.

—*Gene G. Marcial*

INDEX